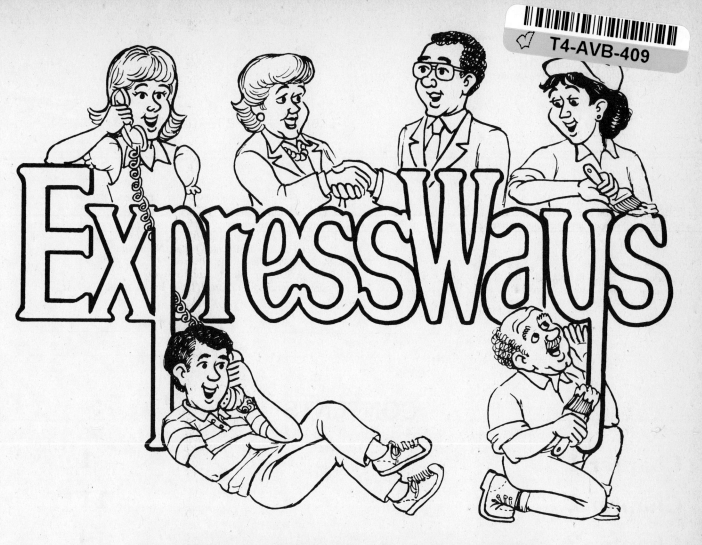

ExpressWays

COMPANION WORKBOOK

1A

Steven J. Molinsky · Bill Bliss

Contributing Author

Ann Kennedy

PRENTICE HALL REGENTS, Englewood Cliffs, NJ 07632

Editorial/production supervision and
    interior design: Louisa B. Hellegers
Development: Ellen Lehrburger
Cover design: Lundgren Graphics Ltd.
Manufacturing buyer: Peter Havens/Arthur P. Michalez

Cover drawing by Gabriel Polonsky

Printed in the United States of America

10 9 8 7 6

ISBN 0-13-298506-3

© 1988 by Prentice-Hall, Inc.
A Division of Simon & Schuster
Englewood Cliffs, New Jersey 07632

Prentice-Hall International (UK) Limited, *London*
Prentice-Hall of Australia Pty. Limited, *Sydney*
Prentice-Hall Canada Inc., *Toronto*
Prentice-Hall Hispanoamericana, S.A., *Mexico*
Prentice-Hall of India Private Limited, *New Delhi*
Prentice-Hall of Japan, Inc., *Tokyo*
Simon & Schuster Asia Pte. Ltd., *Singapore*
Editora Prentice-Hall do Brasil, Ltda., *Rio de Janeiro*

CONTENTS

1

A. WHAT ARE THEY SAYING?

Student Course Book p. 2

meet	Hello	is	you
name	meeting	is My	I'm

1. ___Hello___. My name is Tom.

Hi. My ___name___ is Bill.

2. _____. I'm Jane.

_____ name is Gloria. Nice to

meet _____.

3. Hello. My name _____ Brian.

Hello. _____ Bob.

4. Hi. _____ name is Karen.

Hi. I'm Steve. Nice to _____

you.

5. _____. My _____

_____ Jessica.

Hi. _____ Mary. Nice to

_____ _____.

6. _____. _____ Richard.

Hi. _____ _____

_____ Doris. Nice to

_____ _____.

Nice _____ _____, too.

1

wife   husband

1. I'd like to introduce you to my

   __husband__, George.

2. I'd like to introduce you to my

   _____, Irene.

mother   father

3. I'd like you to meet my

   _____, Mr. Wilson.

4. I'd like to introduce my _____,

   Mrs. Wilson.

brother   sister

5. I'd like to introduce my

   _____, Barbara.

6. This is my _____, Michael.

1. _____
   First   M. I.   Last
                              (Middle Initial)

2. _____
   Last   First   Middle

3. [ ][ ][ ][ ][ ][ ][ ][ ][ ][ ][ ]   [ ][ ][ ][ ][ ][ ][ ][ ]   [ ]
   Last   First   M.I.

4. _____
   Signature

D. LISTENING

Listen and write the missing letters.

1. B r enner   6. __ __ l __ on

2. Barb ___ ra   7. __ __ __ __ rson

3. C ___ ayton   8. M __ __ h __ __ l

4. S ___ ith   9. h __ __ __ __ nd

5. K __ __ n   10. __ __ __ __ __ __ __

Listen and put a circle around the right answer.

1.
| please |
| George |
| (G-R-I-M-E-S) |

4.
| last name |
| Sanchez |
| And you? |

2.
| Barbara |
| brother |
| first |

5.
| Mrs. Chen |
| Linda |
| Hello |

3.
| husband |
| Robert |
| name |

6.
| Clayton |
| last name |
| K-E-L-T-O-N |

F. MISSING LETTERS

Fix the movie sign.

WESTOWN MALL CINEMA

1 MY _AME I_ MICHAEL
2 MY BROT_ER BOB
3 MY S_STER NANCY
4 __EASE!
5 MY __TH_R & F__HER

Fill in the missing letters of the alphabet. Then use the letters to make a word for each group.

1. A B C D E F G H I J K L M N O P Q R S T U V W X Y Z

W I F E

2. ☐ B C D ☐ ☐ G ☐ I J K L M N O P Q ☐ S ☐ U V W X Y Z

☐ ☐ ☐ ☐ ☐ ☐

3. A B C D ☐ F G ☐ I J K L ☐ N ☐ P Q ☐ S ☐ U V W X Y Z

☐ ☐ ☐ ☐ ☐

4. ☐ ☐ C ☐ E F G ☐ I J K L M ☐ O P Q R ☐ T ☐ V W X Y Z

☐ ☐ ☐ ☐ ☐ ☐

Listen and write the number of the address you hear.

1	2	3	4	5	6	7	8	9	10	11	12	13	14	15	16	17	18	19

1. __6__ Maple Street   4. _____ Main Road

2. _____ Pond Avenue   5. _____ Summer Street

3. _____ Howard Street   6. _____ Central Avenue

Listen and write the numbers you hear.

1. 543-690_5_   4. 946-16___ ___

2. 24___-1986   5. ___ ___2-0___ ___7

3. 673-5___ ___0   6. ___ ___ ___-___ ___ ___ ___

Listen and circle the right answer.

1.
| Sanchez. |
| (18 Central Avenue.) |
| 567-0947. |

4.
| 12 Howard Road. |
| Please. |
| Mr. Peterson. |

2.
| 1214 Summer Street. |
| Nice to meet you. |
| 268-5902. |

5.
| 1102 Maple Street. |
| 537-8290. |
| 19. |

3.
| Hi. Nice meeting you. |
| I'm Kim. |
| My name. |

6.
| 10 Main Street. |
| Last name. |
| Grimes. |

K. WHAT'S YOUR NAME? ADDRESS? TELEPHONE NUMBER?   Student Course Book p. 5

1. NAME: _____
            First   M.I.   Last

    ADDRESS: _____
             Number   Street

    TELEPHONE NUMBER: _____ - _____

2. ☐☐☐☐☐☐☐☐☐☐☐   ☐☐☐☐☐☐☐☐☐   ☐
    Last   First   M.I.

    ☐☐☐☐☐☐☐☐☐☐☐☐☐☐☐☐☐☐☐☐☐☐☐☐
    Number   Street

    ☐☐☐☐☐☐☐☐☐☐☐☐☐☐☐☐☐☐☐   ☐☐☐☐☐
    City   State   Zip Code

    ☐☐☐ - ☐☐☐☐
    Telephone Number

I   My

1. __I__'m from New York.

   __My__ name is Michael.

She   Her

2. _____ name is Anna Rossi.

   _____ is from Italy.

We   Our

3. _____ are Miguel and Maria.

   _____ father is Mr. Sanchez.

He   His

4. _____ name is Kenji.

   _____'s from Osaka.

They   Their

5. _____ are Bob and Mary Peterson.

   _____ address is 15 Howard Avenue.

You   Your

6. _____ are Mrs. Wilson.

   _____ first name is Doris.

Put a circle around the letter of the right question.

1.
| a. Where are you from? |
| ⓑ Are you from Osaka? |

No. I'm from Tokyo.

2.
| a. Are you from Italy? |
| b. What's your first name? |

I'm Anna.

3.
| a. Are you Hector? |
| b. Are you from Mexico City? |

No. I'm Miguel.

4.
| a. What's your name? |
| b. Where are you from? |

China.

5.
| a. Are you Mohammed? |
| b. Where are you from? |

Yes. I'm from Egypt.

| he | is | she | their | her |
| your | you | his | they | are |

1. What's ___your___ name?
   My name is Miguel.
   Where ___are___ ___you___
   from?
   Mexico.
2. Where _____ _____
   from?
   He's from Egypt.
   What's _____ name?
   Mohammed.
3. _____ _____ from Canada?
   Yes, he is.
   _____ _____ name David?
   No. His name is Charles.

4. _____ _____ from
   China?
   Yes, they are.
   What _____ _____
   last name?
   Chen.
5. Where _____ _____
   from?
   She's from Italy.
   What's _____ telephone number?
   It's 598-6904.

Listen and circle the best answer.

1.
| a. Yes, I am. |
| b. 10 Main Street. |
| ⓒ I'm from Washington. |

5.
| a. 389. |
| b. N-A-M-E. |
| c. I'm Richard. |

2.
| a. You are. |
| b. Yes, I am. |
| c. Hello. I'm Harry. |

6.
| a. How about you? |
| b. Yes, I am. |
| c. I'm from China. |

3.
| a. No. |
| b. How about you? |
| c. N-E-W Y-O-R-K. |

7.
| a. S-A-N-C-H-E-Z. |
| b. Yes. |
| c. I'm from Puerto Rico. |

4.
| a. N-U-M-B-E-R. |
| b. 678-5520. |
| c. And you? |

8.
| a. Cairo. |
| b. Yes, I am. |
| c. American. |

P. WHO ARE THEY? WHERE ARE THEY FROM?   Student Course Book p. 7

I'm	We're
He's	You're
She's	They're

My	Our
His	Your
Her	Their

1. He's from Mexico City. _____His_____ name is Miguel.

2. _____ last name is Kwan. They're from Beijing.

3. _____ from the Soviet Union. Her mother is Russian.

4. We're from Italy. _____ father is from Rome.

5. _____ American. I'm from New York.

6. You're Mrs. Williams. What is _____ first name, please?

7. I'm Italian. _____ last name is Rossi.

8. They're Australian. _____ from Melbourne.

9. _____ Charles. His wife is Nancy.

10. Our last name is Markova. _____ from Moscow.

Franco is a student in the United States.   He is Italian.   He's from Venice.   His wife is French. Her name is Nicole.   She's from Paris.   Their last name is Rossi.   Their address is 190 Howard Street, San Francisco, California.

Answer the questions.

1. Is Franco from the United States? _____

2. Where is his wife from? _____

3. What's their last name? _____

4. What's her first name? _____

5. What's their address? _____

R.   . . . AND WHAT'S YOUR NATIONALITY?

Fill in the blanks below. Ask for the information from your classmates, your neighbors, or people you work with.

What's your name?   What's your nationality?   What country are you from?   What city are you from?

Name	Nationality	Country	City
Franco Rossi	Italian	Italy	Venice
Harry Miller	American	U.S.	New York

A. MATCHING

Student Course Book p. 10

Draw a line to the correct answer.

1. name — 273-2921
2. street — Mary Hicks
3. city — New York
4. telephone number — Amsterdam Avenue

B. MORE MATCHING

Student Course Book p. 10

1. I'd like the number of — 423-7771.
2. What street? — Sally Craven.
3. The number is — Miami.
4. What city? — C-R-A-V-E-N.
5. How do you spell that? — Harbor Drive.

 ## C. LISTENING

Student Course Book p. 10

Listen and circle the answer to the question.

1. No / (Yes)

Is this 547-2055?

3. No / Yes

624-6835

4. No / Yes

356-9473

2. No / Yes

498-5930

5. No / Yes

285-2841

Listen and write the missing numbers.

1. <u>5 7 3</u> - <u>5 1 0 8</u>

2. __ __ __ - __ __ __ __

3. __ __ __ - __ __ __ __

4. __ __ __ - __ __ __ __

5. __ __ __ - __ __ __ __

6. __ __ __ - __ __ __ __

E. TO BE   Student Course Book p. 11

Am	I	
Is	he she it	} American?
Are	we you they	

1. <u>Are</u> you Japanese?

2. _____ she from Cairo?

3. _____ this 832-1924?

4. _____ they from Mexico?

5. _____ Mr. Carter from New York?

6. _____ he Canadian?

7. _____ your number 349-9654?

8. _____ Alan and Bill your brothers?

9. _____ I on Main Street?

10. _____ we on Hudson Drive?

Write in the correct answer.

No, **I'm not.**	No, $\begin{Bmatrix} he \\ she \\ it \end{Bmatrix}$ **isn't.**	No, $\begin{Bmatrix} we \\ you \\ they \end{Bmatrix}$ **aren't.**

1. Is your husband American?   No, he isn't   .

2. Are your brothers students?   No, _____.

3. Is this 435-9002?   No, _____.

4. Are you Mrs. Wilson?   No, _____.

5. Is this Maple Avenue?   No, _____.

6. Is she your wife?   No, _____.

7. Hello, is this 862-3437?   No, _____.

Fill in the blank with the correct word.

What	How	Where	Are	Is

1. **Where**   are you from?   4. _____ you British?
    New York.   No. I'm Canadian.

2. _____ is your name?   5. _____ this 673-3199?
    Sally.   No. This is 673-3177.

3. _____ do you spell that?   6. _____ they from Miami?
    S-M-I-T-H.   No. They're from Chicago.

am   is   are

1. George ___is___ at the

s u p e r m a r k e t .

2. Mike and Bobby _____ at the

__ __ __ __ __ __ __ .

3. Mr. Nielson _____ at the

__ __ __ __   __ __ __ __ __ __ .

4. I _____ at the

__ __ __ __ __ __ __ __ __ __ .

5. Fred and I _____ at the

__ __ __ __ __ __ __ .

6. You _____ at __ __ __ __ __ __ .

Fill in the signs and answer the questions.

I'm
He's
She's
It's } **going to** the zoo.
We're
You're
They're

1. Where is Susan going?

   She's going to the mall.
   _____

2. Where are Mr. and Mrs. Ingalls going?

   _____

   _____

3. Where are you and your wife going?

   _____

   _____

4. Where is Hector going?

   _____

   _____

5. Where are you going?

   _____

   _____

J. WHAT ARE THEY DOING? I

J. WHAT ARE THEY DOING? I

Student Course Book p. 14

I'm   He's   She's   It's   } going   We're   You're   They're

3. What are you and your husband doing?

_____

1. What's Susan doing?

   She's studying.

4. What are Linda and John doing?

_____

2. What's Mr. Hicks doing?

_____

5. What are you doing?

. . . .

K. WHAT ARE THEY DOING? II

Student Course Book p. 14

I'm   He's   She's   } cleaning   { my / his / her / our / your / their } room.   We're   You're   They're

3. What are you and your brother doing?

_____

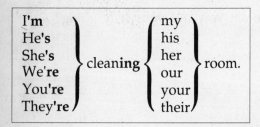

1. What's Melissa doing?

   She's fixing her car.

4. What are you doing?

_____

2. What's Bobby doing?

_____

5. What are the children doing?

_____

16

L. WHAT ARE THEY DOING RIGHT NOW?

Student Course Book p. 15

This is the Henderson family. Paul is _studying_₁. Debbie is _____ _____₂

room. Beth is _____ lunch.₃ Jeff is _____ _____.₄

Mrs. Henderson is_____ on the telephone.₅ Mr. Henderson is _____ his car.₆

M. LISTENING

Student Course Book p. 15

Listen to the conversation and choose the correct picture.

1. ✓

2. _____ _____

3. _____ _____

4. _____ _____

5. _____ _____

6. _____ _____

Steve is calling his friends, but they can't talk right now. His friend Debbie can't talk right now. She's making lunch. His friend Bill can't talk right now. He's cleaning his garage. His friends Melissa and Susan can't talk right now. They're doing their homework. His friend Sally is taking a shower and his friend John is studying.

Steve can't talk to his friends right now. He'll call back later.

Answer the questions.

1. What's Steve doing? <u>He's calling his friends.</u>

2. What's Debbie doing? _____

3. What's Bill doing? _____

4. Are Melissa and Susan cleaning their room? _____

5. What are they doing? _____

6. What's John doing? _____

3

next to	on	across from	around the corner from	between

1. The post office is ___next to___ the clinic.

2. The grocery store is _____ the laundromat and the drug store.

3. The parking lot is _____ Central Avenue.

4. The police station is _____

    _____ the gas station.

5. The museum is _____ the parking lot.

6. The hotel is _____ Main Street.

7. The clinic is _____ the post office and the grocery store.

8. The bank is _____ the fire station.

Is there	across from	next to	between
There's	around the corner from	on	

1. Excuse me. __Is there__ a clinic nearby?

    Yes. _____ a clinic _____ River Street.

2. _____ a post office nearby?

    Yes. It's _____ Main Street, _____ the bank.

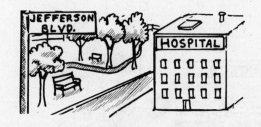

3. Is there a bus station _____ Grand Avenue?

    Yes. _____ a bus station _____ the laundromat.

4. _____ a hospital nearby?

    Yes. _____ a hospital _____ Jefferson Boulevard.

5. Excuse me. _____ a hotel nearby?

    Yes. It's _____ Main Street, _____ the post office.

6. _____ a police station nearby?

    Yes. _____ a police station _____ the gas station.

C. WHERE DOES IT GO?

| Does | this ship
this plane
this train
this bus
it | go to New York? |

Yes, it does.
No, it doesn't.

It goes to Boston.

1. Does this ship __go__ to Puerto Rico?   Yes, __it does__.

2. _____ this plane _____ to the Bahamas?   No, _____.

_____ to Puerto Rico.

3. _____ Bus Number 48 _____ to the Bronx?   Yes, _____.

4. _____ this train go uptown?   No, _____.

_____ downtown.

5. _____ it _____ to Italy?   No, _____.

_____ to Mexico.

D. LISTENING

Listen to each conversation. Put a circle around the number you hear.

1. (29) / 39
2. 34 / 43
3. 56 / 35
4. 12 / 20
5. 68 / 78
6. 72 / 73
7. 58 / 75
8. 4936 / 7947
9. 5416 / 4560
10. 6846 / 8646
11. 4028 / 1482
12. 5764 / 5774

| Is this Bus Number 42? | Yes, it is.
No, it isn't. |

| Does this plane go to Florida? | Yes, it does.
No, it doesn't. |

1. Is this the bus to Florida?   Yes, _it is_ .

2. Does this train go downtown?   No, _____ .

3. Is this your telephone number?   No, _____ .

4. Does it stop at Broadway?   Yes, _____ .

5. Is this the bus to the mall?   Yes, _____ .

F.   LISTENING   Student Course Book p. 21

Listen to each question. Put a circle around the correct answer.

1.
   a. Yes, it is.
   b. Yes, it does.

5.
   a. Yes, it is.
   b. Yes, it does.

2.
   a. No, it doesn't.
   b. No, it isn't.

6.
   a. No, it doesn't.
   b. No, it isn't.

3.
   a. Yes, it does.
   b. Yes, it is.

7.
   a. Yes, it does.
   b. Yes, it is.

4.
   a. No, it isn't.
   b. No, it doesn't.

8.
   a. No, it isn't.
   b. No, it doesn't.

left	next to
right	across from
	between

1. Excuse me. Can you tell me how to get to the hospital?

    Yes. Walk THAT way. It's on the <u>right</u>.

2. How do I get to the Empire Hotel?

    It's on the _____.

3. Where's the parking lot?

    It's on the _____.

4. Is there a post office nearby?

    Yes, there is. The post office is on

    the _____ , _____

    the supermarket.

5. Can you tell me how to get to the bank?

    Yes. Walk THAT way. It's on the _____ , _____ the supermarket.

6. Where's the library?

    It's on the _____ , _____ the supermarket and the hospital.

7. Is there a department store nearby?

    Yes. It's on the _____ , _____ the Empire Hotel.

8. How do I get to the bus station?

    Walk THAT way. It's on the _____ , _____ the post office and the

    parking lot.

Listen to each sentence. Put the number of the sentence in the correct box.

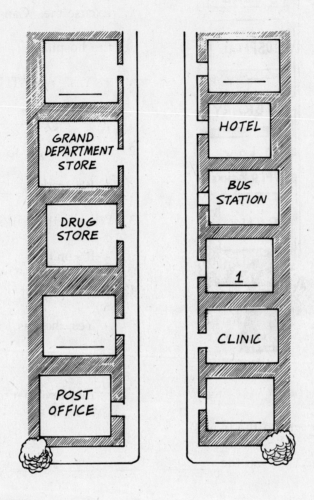

Draw a line to the correct answer.

1. Walk   two blocks.

2. Turn   the library on the right.

3. Go   that way to Second Avenue.

4. Look for   your name.

5. Write   left.

Walk	Turn	Look for

1. ___Turn___ left.

2. _____ two blocks to Oak Street.

3. _____ the train station on the right.

4. _____ right on Third Avenue.

5. _____ that way to Fifth Avenue.

walk	turn	look for	left	right	block

Excuse me. Can you tell me how to get to the police station?

Yes. ___Walk___ that way on First Avenue. Then _____ right on Pine Street.
1   2

_____ two blocks and _____ the police station on the _____.
3   4   5

How do I get to the post office?

_____ that way to Third Avenue and turn _____. Go one _____
6   7   8

and _____ the post office on the _____.
9   10

Unscramble the sentences.

1. you   much   very   Thank

   <u>Thank you very much.</u>

2. First   to   blocks   Go   Avenue   two

   _____

3. me   museum   get   Can   to   to   you   how   tell   the

   _____

4. say   First   Did   Avenue   you

   _____

5. right   That's

   _____

Now write the conversation in the correct order below.

_____

_____

_____

_____

_____

Listen to each conversation. Put a circle around the correct answer.

1. | Yes   (No) | 6. | Yes   No |

2. | Yes   No | 7. | Yes   No |

3. | Yes   No | 8. | Yes   No |

4. | Yes   No | 9. | Yes   No |

5. | Yes   No | 10. | Yes   No |

N. MATCHING

1. Drive ———————————————— right on Third Street.

2. Take ————————————————————— ten miles.

3. Get off   the gas station on the left.

4. Turn   at the first exit.

5. Look for   this bus and get off at Summer Street.

 ## O. LISTENING

Write the number of the location you hear.

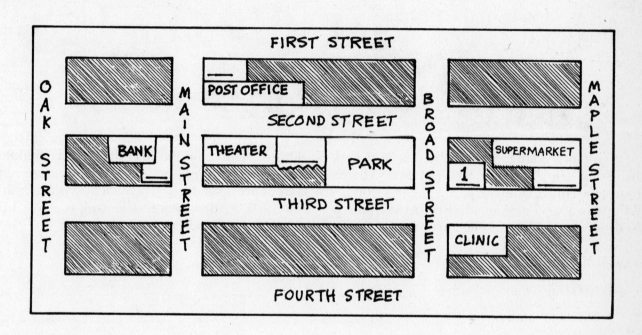

P. TURN RIGHT!

at	on	to	for	from

1. Turn right ____on____ Oak Road.

2. This bus goes _____ Westville.

3. He's _____ the bank now.

4. Can you tell me how to get _____ the Grand Hotel?

5. I'm looking _____ John. Is he here?

6. It's across _____ the library.

7. The bus stop is _____ Spring Street.

8. Get off the Expressway _____ Exit 16.

Excuse me. Can you tell me how to get to your home? (Write directions from your school to where you live.)

Yes. . . . .

. . . .

. . . .

. . . .

. . . .

R.   READING: *Janet's Neighborhood*   Student Course Book p. 25

I'm Janet Warner. My address is 5432 Park Boulevard. I live on the fifth floor of my building. This is my neighborhood. It's very nice. There's a park across from my building. There's a museum around the corner from the park. The bus stop is across from my apartment. There's a post office nearby and there's a very nice laundromat between the post office and the drug store. The bank is across from the drug store. I like my neighborhood very much. It's very nice and everything is nearby.

Answer the questions.

1.   What's the woman's name? _____

2.   What's her address? _____

3.   What floor does she live on? _____

4.   Is her neighborhood nice? _____

5.   Where's the park? _____

6.   What's around the corner from the park? _____

7.   Where's the bus stop? _____

8.   Is there a zoo nearby? _____

9.   Where's the laundromat? _____

10. What's next to the drug store? _____

11. Where's the bank? _____

12. Does Janet like her neighborhood? _____

13. Now tell about YOUR neighborhood. . . . .

. . . .

. . . .

A. Answer the questions.

1. What's your name?

. . . .

2. What's your address?

. . . .

3. Where are you from?

. . . .

4. What's your telephone number?

. . . .

B. Put a circle around the correct answer.

Example   Peter is my
| wife |
| American |
| (brother) |
.

1. Is your sister there?

No,
| they're |
| he's |
| she's |
at the post office.

2. I'm fixing my
| address |
| today |
| bicycle |
.

3. Timmy is at the library.

He's
| studying |
| fixing |
| going |
.

4. We're
| cleaning |
| doing |
| watching |
our homework.

5.
| Go |
| Going |
| Goes |
three blocks and turn right.

6.
| Does |
| There's |
| Is there |
a clinic nearby?

7.
| Is |
| Does |
| Is there |
this plane go to Miami?

8.
| Where |
| What |
| Can |
are you doing?

9. I'm going
| at |
| for |
| to |
the park.

10.
| Am |
| Is |
| Are |
Melissa and Janet there?

11.
| Are |
| Is |
| Does |
this bus stop at the mall?

C. Fill in the blanks.

Example _____How_____ are you?
        Fine.

1. _____ Patty doing?
   She's studying.

2. _____ are they going?
   To the beach.

3. _____ do I get to the
   expressway?
   Drive that way.

4. _____ are they doing?
   They're watching TV.

D. Fill in the blanks.

Example Where _____does_____ this bus go?

1. Where _____ he?

2. Where _____ I get off?

3. Where _____ you going?

4. Where _____ they from?

5. Where _____ this train stop?

E. Answer the questions.

Example Where's Janet?

She's at the laundromat.

2. What's Steve doing?

_____

1. Where are Fred and Jimmy?

_____

3. What are you doing?

_____

F. Listen and write the number you hear.

Example _____56_____

1. _____

2. _____

3. _____

4. _____

5. _____

6. _____

7. _____

8. _____

9. _____

30

4

A. WHERE IS EVERYBODY?

Student Course Book p. 30

| I'm   She's   We're | dining room   bedroom   bathroom |
| He's   They're | living room   kitchen |

1. Where is Sally?

   ___She's___ in the **bedroom** .

2. Where are Bill and Timmy?

   _____ in the _____.

3. Where are Mr. and Mrs. Smith?

   _____ in the _____.

4. Where is Carlos?

   _____ in the _____.

5. Where are you and Janet?

   _____ in the _____.

6. Where are you?

   _____ in the _____.

B. YES, THERE IS

Student Course Book p. 31

| Yes, there is. | Yes, there are. |
| No, there isn't. | No, there aren't. |

1. Is there a shower in the bathroom?   Yes, ___there is_____.

2. Are there cabinets in the kitchen?   Yes, _____.

3. Is there a fireplace?   No, _____.

4. Are there elevators in the building?   No, _____.

5. Is there a dishwasher?   Yes, _____.

31

Listen to each conversation. Put the number in the appropriate place.

D. IS OR DOES?   Student Course Book p. 32

is	does

1. How much ____is____ the rent?

2. _____ that include utilities?

3. How much _____ the parking fee?

4. _____ that include gas?

5. _____ there a closet in the bathroom?

6. _____ there a refrigerator?

7. _____ the rent include heat?

8. _____ there a bus stop on Main Street?

E. MATCHING   Student Course Book p. 32

1. Do you want to see the apartment?   Yes, there is.

2. How much is the rent?   Four.

3. Does that include heat?   Yes, I do.

4. How many windows are there?   No, it doesn't.

5. Is there an elevator?   It's $650.

Listen to each sentence. Put the number under the appropriate box.

3 BEDROOM APARTMENT $580	APARTMENT FOR RENT $225	APARTMENT $650 PLUS UTILITIES	APARTMENT $430	2 BEDROOM APARTMENT 978-6229

_____   _____   _____   _____1_____   _____

Listen to each conversation. Write the number you hear.

1. $ _600_____   3. $ _____   5. $ _____

2. $ _____   4. _____   6. _____

H.   *THIS* OR *THESE*?   Student Course Book p. 33

1. Where do you want ___this___ bed?   4. _____ kitchen is very nice.

2. Put _____ lamps in the bedroom.   5. _____ tables? Put them in the living room.

3. And how about _____ plant?

I.   *THAT* OR *THOSE*?   Student Course Book p. 33

1. ___That___ rug? Put it in the bathroom.   4. _____ bedroom has three closets.

2. _____ pictures are very nice.   5. Do you want to see _____ apartment?

3. Where do you want _____ chairs?

J.   WHERE DO YOU WANT THESE PICTURES?   Student Course Book p. 33

this	that	these	those

1. Where do you want ___these___ pictures?   3. And how about _____ rug?

2. _____ pictures? Put them on the table.   4. _____ rug? Please put it in the living room.

K. HOW ABOUT THOSE CHAIRS?

picture chairs

1. Where do you want those __chairs__ ?

sofa tables

4. Put this _____ in the living room.

name words

2. How do you spell this _____?

building apartments

5. Do you want to see that _____?

bedroom apartments

3. Are there waterbeds in those

_____?

kitchen bedrooms

6. This _____ is large.

L. LISTENING

Listen to each sentence. Put a check (✓) under the appropriate picture.

1.

2. ✓

3.

4.

5.

6.

M. A OR AN?

a cookie	an apple
a tomato	an egg

1. __a__ banana   4. _____ bus   7. _____ apartment   10. _____ egg

2. _____ orange   5. _____ stove   8. _____ expressway   11. _____ rug

3. _____ elevator   6. _____ apple   9. _____ shower   12. _____ exit

N. AN APPLE OR APPLES?

Student Course Book p. 34

1. an apple   _apples_
2. _____ eggs
3. a banana _____
4. _____ oranges

5. _____ cookies
6. a tomato _____
7. a closet _____
8. _____ elevators

O. LISTENING

Student Course Book p. 34

Listen to each sentence. Put a circle around the word you hear.

1. tomato   (tomatoes)
2. refrigerator   refrigerators
3. egg   eggs
4. cookie   cookies
5. banana   bananas

6. apple   apples
7. orange   oranges
8. chair   chairs
9. neighborhood   neighborhoods
10. elevator   elevators

P. IS THERE ANY MILK?

Student Course Book p. 35

isn't	aren't

1. I'm afraid there ___isn't___ any more milk.
2. There _____ any eggs.
3. There _____ any more coffee.
4. I'm afraid there _____ any nice tomatoes.
5. There _____ any lettuce in the refrigerator.

6. There _____ any more cookies in the kitchen.
7. I'm sorry. There _____ any more bread.
8. I'm afraid there _____ any more ice cream.
9. There _____ any cheese.
10. There _____ any more oranges.

Q. I'M LOOKING FOR A COOKIE

Student Course Book p. 35

1. I'm looking for a (cookie/cheese).
2. I'll get some (tomato/tomatoes).
3. There isn't any more (coffee/egg).

4. There aren't any (bread/apples).
5. I'll get some (lettuce/orange).
6. There isn't any (milk/cookies).

is	It's
are	They're

1. Where _____is_____ the rice?

   _____ in Aisle 9.

2. Where _____ the potatoes?

   _____ in Aisle F.

3. Where _____ the peaches?

   _____ in Aisle J.

4. Where _____ the sugar?

   _____ in Aisle D.

Listen to each sentence. Put a circle around the correct answer.

1. (8)   H   4.   E   G   7.   A   J

2. B   D   5.   3   C   8.   16   10C

3. N   M   6.   9   19   9.   18   8D

Draw a line to the correct response for each pair.

1. These peaches are delicious!   I'm glad you like it.

2. This cake is delicious!   I'm glad you like them.

3. Excuse me. Where is the sugar?   It's in the cabinet.

4. Where are the eggs?   They're in the refrigerator.

5. I'm afraid there isn't any more coffee.   There aren't?

6. There aren't any more carrots.   There isn't?

7. Where do you want this TV?   Put them in the living room.

8. Where do you want these plants?   Put it in the living room.

This	is	it	it's
These	are	them	they're

1. Mmm! ___These___ cookies

   _____ delicious!

   I'm glad you like _____.

   What's in _____?

   Raisins, eggs, sugar, butter, and flour.

   _____ excellent!

   Thank you.

2. Mmm! _____ yogurt is delicious!

   I'm glad you like _____.

   What's in _____?

   Apples and raisins.

   _____ excellent!

   Thanks.

V.   READING: *Jim's New Apartment*   Student Course Book p. 37

Jim has a new apartment near the university. He's showing his new apartment to his friend Tom. The apartment has a living room with a large window. There is a very large kitchen with a dishwasher and many cabinets. There is a shower in the bathroom and the bedroom has a nice large closet. The rent is $450 a month and that includes utilities.

Tom is looking for a new apartment. There are two vacant apartments in the building. Jim might have a new neighbor!

Answer these questions.

1. Where is Jim's new apartment? _____

   _____

2. Is there a large window in the living room? _____

   _____

3. Can you describe Jim's kitchen? _____

   _____

4. Are there two closets in the bedroom? _____

   _____

5. What is the rent? _____

   Does it include utilities? _____

6. Does Tom want to see the vacant apartments? _____

5

A. CAN THEY COOK?
Student Course Book p. 40

I He She We You They	**can** cook.

1. She can fix cars.

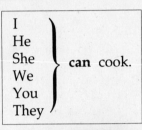

2. _____

3. _____

4. _____

5. _____

6. _____

B. YES, THEY CAN

Student Course Book p. 40

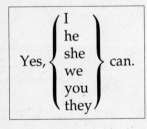

Yes, { I he she we you they } can.

cashier	dishwasher	housekeeper
cook	mechanic	stock clerk

1. Can you use a cash register?

    Yes, I can .

    I'm a cashier .

2. Can your brother fix cars?

    Yes, _____.

    He's a _____.

3. Can Maria clean rooms and make beds?

    Yes, _____.

    She's a _____.

4. Can Natasha make sandwiches?

    Yes, _____.

    She's a _____.

5. Can those men lift heavy boxes?

    Yes, _____.

    They're _____.

6. Can you and Anna operate kitchen equipment?

    Yes, _____.

    We're _____.

38

C. WHAT TIME IS IT?

  It's 10:00.   It's 9:30.   It's 6:00.    It's 1:30.

Write the correct time under each clock.

1. __It's 6:30.__   2. _____   3. _____   4. _____   5. _____

D. DO YOU HAVE THE TIME?

Draw the time on the clocks.

  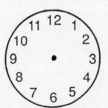 

1. It's 2:00.   2. It's 3:30.   3. It's 7:30.   4. It's 9:00.

E. ON THURSDAY AT 10:00

MONDAY	TUESDAY	WEDNESDAY	THURSDAY	FRIDAY	SATURDAY
1:30 KAREN PETERSON	9:30 PETER HALL 10:00 DORIS CLAYTON	2:30 BARBARA WARNER	10:00 BRENDA TAYLOR 1:00 GEORGE SMITH	3:00 SUSAN TYLER	

1. Brenda Taylor's interview is on ___Thursday___ at ___10:00___.

2. Peter Hall has an interview on _____ at _____.

3. Barbara Warner's interview is on _____ at _____.

4. Karen Peterson is coming in for an interview on _____ at _____.

5. Susan Tyler is coming in for an interview on _____ at _____.

6. Doris Clayton has an interview on _____ at _____.

7. George Smith's interview is on _____ at _____.

F. LISTENING

Listen to each sentence. Put a circle around the correct day or time.

1.
12:00
(2:00)

3.
8:00
3:00

5.
Monday
Sunday

2.
10:30
10:00

4.
Tuesday
Thursday

6.
Tuesday at 2:00
Thursday at 3:00

G. LISTENING

Listen and write the time you hear.

1. 8:30   3. _____   5. _____

2. _____   4. _____   6. _____

H. I CAN DO IT!

actor	medical technician	custodian	secretary	data processor
chef	lab technician	mechanic	driver	office assistant

1. I can operate X-ray equipment. I'm a very experienced ___medical technician___.

2. She can type and take shorthand. She's a good _____.

3. Hector can sing and dance very well. He's a very good _____.

4. My brothers can fix cars. They're very good _____.

5. I know how to operate office equipment. I'm a very good _____.

6. They can use computers. They're _____.

7. Mr. Wilson can use cleaning equipment. He can operate a heating system, too. He's an

experienced _____.

8. We can prepare international food and we know how to cook American food. We're

experienced _____.

9. They can use laboratory equipment. They're very good _____.

10. Norman Johnson can drive trucks. He's an experienced _____.

I. OCCUPATIONS AND SKILLS

Student Course Book p. 42

Draw a line from the occupation to the appropriate skill.

1. chef   operate kitchen equipment
2. custodian   sing, dance
3. medical technician   lift heavy boxes
4. secretary   prepare international food
5. actor   take blood
6. sales clerk   take inventory
7. dishwasher   take shorthand
8. stock clerk   repair things

J. NO, I CAN'T

Student Course Book p. 43

1. Can you type?

   No, ___I can't___ .

2. Can Gary and Peter use lab equipment?

   No, _____ .

3. Can Barbara talk to customers?

   No, _____ .

4. Can George use word processing equipment?

   No, _____ .

5. Can they use a computer?

   No, _____ .

6. Can you and I speak Russian?

   No, _____ .

K. WHAT'S THE OCCUPATION?

Student Course Book p. 43

| secretary   office assistant   custodian   waiter   sales clerk |

1. Can you use a copying machine? We need a good ___office assistant___ .

2. I can operate a heating system. I'm an experienced _____ .

3. Can you take orders and make salads? We really need a good _____ .

4. Can you take inventory and use a cash register? We need an experienced _____ .

5. Can you type well? We need an experienced _____ .

L. THESE PEOPLE ARE EMPLOYED

I
You
We } work at the Crown Insurance Company.
You
They

He
She } works at the Crown Insurance Company.

I'm
You're } a typist.

We're
You're } typists.
They're

He's
She's } a typist.

1. [I / I'm] a security guard.

2. [He / He's] works at Tyler School.

3. [You / You're] an excellent waiter.

4. [She / She's] helps customers.

5. [They / They're] teachers.

6. [We / We're] fix cars at Auto World.

M. WHAT'S THE JOB?

Write sentences about these people.

| custodian | data processor | office assistant | ESL teacher | mechanic |
| waitress | medical technician | science teacher | secretary | cook |

1. Mr. Peterson teaches Biology. ___He's a science teacher.___

2. Gary takes blood. _____

3. Mrs. Johnson types well. _____

4. Mr. Ling uses a computer. _____

5. Jim Warner teaches English. _____

6. Mr. Wilson repairs things. _____

7. Ann works at a restaurant. _____

8. Norman makes eggs and sandwiches. _____

9. She operates office equipment. _____

10. Gary fixes cars. _____

N. I STOCK THE SHELVES

Put a circle around the correct word.

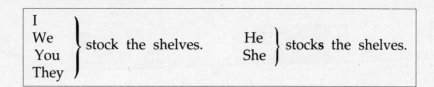

1. I (clean) / cleans rooms.

2. We take / takes orders.

3. He drive / drives a truck.

4. A medical technician take / takes blood.

5. Security guards check / checks I.D. cards.

6. That waitress make / makes salads well.

O. WHAT DO THEY DO?

Fill in the blanks.

1. A stock clerk __takes__ inventory.

2. Custodians _____ things.

3. A salesperson _____ customers.

4. I _____ office equipment.

5. Karen _____ rock 'n roll.

6. Gary and Jeff _____ computers.

7. We _____ salads.

8. She _____ shorthand.

P. MATCHING

1. I'm an excellent housekeeper. I   helps customers in a store.

2. Maria is a waitress. She   do lab tests.

3. He's a salesperson. He   guard the building entrance.

4. Medical technicians   serves food in a restaurant.

5. Those security guards   clean rooms in a hotel.

Q. MONEY, MONEY, MONEY Student Course Book p. 46

Write the correct amount under the picture.

| $1.00 | $5.00 | $10.00 | $50,000 |

1. $5.00
2. _____
3. _____
4. _____

R. LISTENING Student Course Book p. 46

Listen to each conversation. Write the number you hear.

1. $ 6.00 an hour
2. $_____ an hour
3. At _____

4. $_____ a week
5. $_____ a year
6. At _____

7. From _____ to _____
8. From _____ to _____
9. From _____ to _____

S. WHAT'S THE SCHEDULE? Student Course Book p. 46

| Hours **at** the office are **from** 9:00 **to** 5:30. |

| to   from   at |

1. Hours are from 8:30 ___to___ 4:00.

2. Lunch is _____ 12:30 to 1:00.

3. The work schedule is _____ 6:30 _____ 3:00.

4. The lunch break at the restaurant is _____ 11:30.

5. Our hours are _____ 4:00 _____ 12:00.

6. His break is _____ 10:30.

T. LISTENING Student Course Book p. 46

Listen to each sentence. Put a circle around the correct answer.

1.	5:00	($5.00)		5.	11:00	$11.00
2.	12:00	$12.00		6.	5:00	$50.00
3.	2:30	$230.00		7.	3:30	$3.30
4.	4:00	$4.00		8.	1:00	$1.00

U. WHAT DO YOUR FRIENDS DO?

waiter	data processor
custodian	medical technician
dishwasher	sales clerk

| operate | take |
| operates | takes |

1. Kenji is a _____waiter_____. He _____takes_____ orders.

2. Carlos and Kim are _____. They _____ heating equipment.

3. Maria and Mei _____ inventory. They're _____.

4. Paolo and Anna are _____. They _____ computers.

5. My friend is a _____. He _____ kitchen equipment.

6. I'm a _____. I _____ X-ray equipment.

V. READING: *A Job Interview*

Susan doesn't have a job right now. She's looking for a job as a secretary in New York. She has a job interview on Friday at 2:00. She has good skills. She can file, type, and operate office equipment. She can use a copying machine, but she can't use word processing equipment. She's from Mexico. She was the manager of an office in Mexico City for three years. She can speak English well. She can't write reports well in English, but she's sure she can learn quickly. The hours for the job are 9:00 to 5:00, but she doesn't know the salary.

Susan is very confident. She is positive she can get this position!

Answer the questions.

1. Is Susan currently employed? ___No, she isn't._____

2. What's Susan looking for? _____

3. When is her interview? _____

4. What are her skills? _____

5. Where is she originally from? _____

6. What was her position there? _____

7. How long did she work at that office? _____

8. Can she speak English well? _____

9. Can she write reports well in English? _____

10. What are the hours for the job? _____

11. What's the salary? _____

12. Is she sure she can get the job? _____

A. YOU DON'T LOOK VERY WELL

Student Course Book p. 50

I		
You	} have	
		a stomachache.
He		
She	} has	

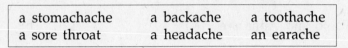

a stomachache   a backache   a toothache
a sore throat   a headache   an earache

1. What's the matter with you?

   I have a backache.

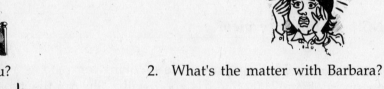

2. What's the matter with Barbara?

   _____

3. What's the matter with Mr. Johnson?

   _____

4. What's the matter with you?

   _____

5. What's the matter with him?

   _____

6. What's the matter with me?

   _____

 ## B. LISTENING

Student Course Book p. 50

Listen to each sentence. Write the correct number under the appropriate picture.

___   ___   ___   ___   ___   _1_

C. WHAT'S THE MATTER?

Student Course Book p. 50

I You } **have** a backache.	He She } **has** a backache.
We You They } **have** backaches.	

1. My brother ___has___ an earache.

2. I _____ a toothache.

3. You _____ a sore throat.

4. Carmen and Jessica _____ stomachaches.

5. Anna and I _____ headaches.

6. Rick _____ a backache.

D. CAN YOU HELP ME?

Student Course Book p. 51

it	them
It's	They're

1. I recommend cold medicine.

   Where can I find ___it___ ?

2. Where can I find aspirin?

   _____ in Aisle 3.

3. I recommend ear drops.

   Where can I find _____?

4. Where can I find throat lozenges?

   _____ in Aisle 1.

5. Where can I find cough syrup?

   _____ in Aisle 6.

6. I recommend tablets.

   Where can I find _____?

E. MY MEDICINE CABINET

Student Course Book p. 51

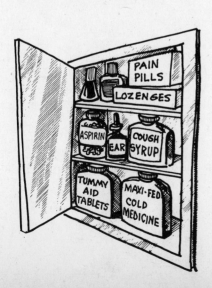

top	middle	bottom

1. The ear drops are on the ___middle___ shelf.

2. Maxi-Fed Cold Medicine is on the _____ shelf.

3. The aspirin is on the _____ shelf.

4. There are throat lozenges on the _____ shelf.

5. The medicine for stomachaches is on the _____ shelf.

47

F. ON THE DRUG STORE SHELF

Student Course Book p. 51

> back   front   near   in   on

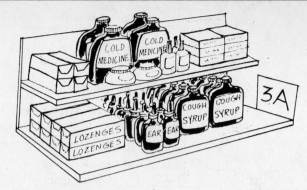

1. The cough syrup is ___on___ the right.

2. The cold medicine is in the _____.

3. There are ear drops in the _____.

4. The lozenges are _____ the ear drops.

5. These items are _____ Aisle 3A.

G. WHAT DO YOU SUGGEST?

Student Course Book p. 51

Draw a line to the correct suggestion.

1. I have a bad headache.   I recommend Drum's Ear Drops.

2. She has a terrible stomachache.   I recommend Taylor's Aspirin.

3. Johnny has an earache.   I recommend this cough syrup.

4. I have a bad cough.   I recommend these pain pills.

5. Mr. Chen has a backache.   I recommend Tummy Aid Tablets.

H. IT'S 9:15

Student Course Book p. 52

It's 9:15.

It's 10:45.

It's 3:45.

It's 6:15.

Write the time under the clock.

1. 11:45   2. _____   3. _____   4. _____   5. _____

I. LISTENING: *Can You Come in at 10:15?*

Student Course Book p. 52

Listen to each question. Write the time you hear.

1. 10:15   3. _____   5. _____

2. _____   4. _____   6. _____

Listen to each sentence. Put the number under the appropriate box.

__1__ ___ ___ ___ ___

K. SOME QUESTIONS

Fill in the blanks.

| Are | Is | Do | Does |

1. __Are__ you feeling okay?

2. _____ you have an earache?

3. _____ you drink?

4. _____ he have a toothache?

5. _____ there a history of allergies in your family?

6. _____ you feeling dizzy?

7. _____ there any more pills?

8. _____ Mr. Smith smoke?

L. SOME ANSWERS

| I do | I am | there is | there are |
| I don't | I'm not | there isn't | there aren't |

1. Are you feeling well?

    No, __I'm not_____.

2. Are you feeling dizzy?

    Yes, _____.

3. Do you have an earache?

    Yes, _____.

4. Do you drink?

    No, _____.

5. Is there a history of heart disease in your family?

    No, _____.

6. Are there any more tablets?

    Yes, _____.

7. Is there any medicine for this allergy?

    Yes, _____.

8. Are there any more questions?

    No, _____.

M. A DOCTOR'S APPOINTMENT

Write the number of the instruction next to the correct picture.

1. Hold your breath.	3. Sit on the table.	5. Say "a-a-h"!
2. Take off your shirt.	4. Roll up your sleeve.	6. Cough.

 ___    ___   ___

 ___    ___    ___

Practice giving and following these instructions with another student.

N. MY TOES?

Draw a line to complete the sentence.

1. Touch   the ceiling.

2. Roll up   on your back.

3. Hold   your toes.

4. Lie   your sleeve.

5. Look at   your breath.

O. I'M CONCERNED

I	
He	
She	**should** go on a diet.
We	
You	
They	

stop eating salty foods
do sit-ups
go on diets
use dental floss daily
quit smoking immediately

1. I'm concerned about your blood pressure. You _should stop eating salty foods_.

2. I'm concerned about his back. He _____.

3. I'm concerned about their gums. They _____.

4. I'm concerned about her lungs. She _____.

5. I'm concerned about our weight. We _____.

P. THE DOCTOR'S ADVICE

Put a circle around the correct answer.

Metropolitan Separate School Board
Continuing Education Dept.
ADULT ENGLISH CLASSES

1. I suggest that you lose 15 pounds. You should

    | slow down |
    | (go on a diet) |
    .

2. I'm concerned about his blood pressure. He should

    | change his diet |
    | use dental floss |
    .

3. I'm concerned about your lungs. You should

    | quit smoking |
    | take a vacation |
    .

4. I'm concerned about their gums. They should

    | do sit-ups |
    | use dental floss |
    .

5. I'm concerned about your back. You should

    | stop eating |
    | exercise daily |
    .

Q. MATCHING

Draw a line to the correct label.

one tablet = 1 tab.	once a day = 1X/day
two capsules = 2 caps.	twice a day = 2X/day
three teaspoons = 3 tsps.	three times a day = 3X/day

1. Take two capsules three times a day.   3 tabs. 2X/day

2. Take three tablets twice a day.   2 tsps. 3X/day

3. Take one pill four times a day.   2 caps. 3X/day

4. Take two teaspoons three times a day.   3 tsps. 2X/day

5. Take three teaspoons twice a day.   1 pill 4X/day

R. FOLLOW THE DIRECTIONS

Write the instructions in the short form.

1. Take three pills three times a day.   _3 pills 3X/day_

2. Take two tablets twice a day.   _____

3. Take one capsule once a day.   _____

4. Take one teaspoon two times a day.   _____

Listen to the directions. Put the number under the appropriate medicine bottle.

1

_____   _____   _____   _____   _____   _____

T. MATCHING   Student Course Book p. 57

Draw a line to complete the sentence.

1. My mother is having   in my house.

2. I think my house is   breathe.

3. My husband can't   on fire.

4. I think there's a burglar   right away.

5. We'll be there   a heart attack.

U. READING: *Call 911*   Student Course Book p. 57

Carol Davis is an operator, but she doesn't work at the telephone company. She works at the Police Emergency Unit in her city. People call "9-1-1" and speak to her when they want to report an emergency.

Carol is very busy right now. A man thinks there is a burglar in his apartment. He's telling Carol his name, address, and telephone number.

Diane Stewart also works at the Police Emergency Unit. She's very busy, too. A woman is reporting a medical emergency. The woman's husband is having a heart attack. Diane is calling the hospital. An ambulance will be there right away.

Now somebody is reporting a *new* emergency to Carol. An apartment building is on fire! Carol is calling the fire department. They'll be there right away.

Carol and Diane like their jobs. They like to help people, and their work is very exciting.

Answer the questions.

1. What's Carol's occupation? _____

2. Where does she work? _____

3. What number do people call to report an emergency? _____

4. Is Carol busy now? _____

5. What's the man's problem? _____

6. Where does Diane Stewart work? _____

7. What's the woman reporting? _____

8. What's Diane doing? _____

9. What's on fire? _____

10. Do Carol and Diane like their jobs? _____

    Why? _____

A. Put a circle around the correct answer.

Example

I
I do
(I'm)

married.

7. A waiter

serves
serving
serve

the food.

1.

Are
Can
Do

you help me?

8. There

has
is
are

a position at the bank.

2. I can come in

on
at
to

Monday.

9. Can you come

from
to
at

12:30?

3. The salary is $200

for
a
one

week.

10. I'm looking for an

apartment
capsule
ear drops

.

4. Where are

the
that
an

ads?

11. This is my

sons
husbands
daughter

.

5. Henry

does
is
has

a backache.

12.

Looking
Lies
Sit

on the table.

6.

May
Can
Know

you use a typewriter?

13. What

are
do
is

your position?

B. Answer the questions.

Example   Is she currently employed?   Yes, __she is__.

1. Can you do lab tests?   Yes, _____.

2. Do you have a daughter?   No, _____.

3. Are they experienced waiters?   Yes, _____.

4. Is there an elevator in this building?   No _____.

5. Does Neal have a stomachache?   Yes, _____.

C. Fill in the blanks.

Example ___Is___ there a problem?

1. _____ you smoke?

2. _____ you dizzy?

3. _____ you allergic to this medicine?

4. _____ that include electricity?

5. _____ there any more eggs?

6. _____ he bleeding?

7. _____ there a history of heart disease in your family?

D. Put a circle around the word that doesn't belong.

Example apple   (beach)   tomato   bread

1. daughter   doctor   brother   mother

2. type   waiter   cashier   manager

3. aspirin   ear drops   gums   cough medicine

4. those   this   these   their

E. Answer the questions.

Example   What's she looking for?

She's looking for rice.

1. What does a salesperson do?

_____

2. What's the matter with you?

_____

3. What should the woman do?

_____

F. Listen and write the number you hear.

Example $ 300

1. _____ caps.

2. _____ : _____

3. $ _____ a year

4. _____ years

5. _____ Park Lane

6. Aisle _____

7. _____ bedrooms

8. _____ : _____

9. $ _____ a month

7

A. THIS DRESS IS NICE

Student Course Book p. 62

Put a circle around the correct word.

1. This ⟨dress⟩ / dresses is nice.

2. Where are the coat / coats ?

3. I'm looking for a hat / hats .

4. Umbrella / Umbrellas are on that table.

5. I recommend this tie / ties with that shirt.

6. Blouses / Blouse are on that rack.

B. SINGULAR/PLURAL

Student Course Book p. 62

1. a coat   coats

2. _____ blouses

3. a dress _____

4. _____ hats

5. a shirt _____

6. a tie _____

7. _____ umbrellas

8. a shoe _____

C. KAREN'S SUITCASE

Student Course Book p. 62

Karen is going to New York tomorrow. What is she packing in her suitcase?

a. _a dress_

b. _____

c. _____

d. _____

e. _____

f. _____

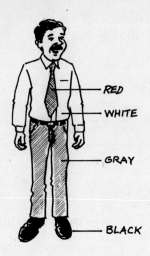

1. What's Mr. Peterson wearing?

   He's wearing _a white shirt,_
   _____
   _____
   _____

2. What's Mrs. Peterson wearing?

   She's wearing _____
   _____
   _____
   _____

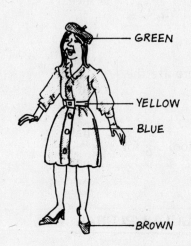

3. What are you wearing today?

   . . . .

   . . . .

   . . . .

 E. LISTENING: *I'm Looking for a Sweater*   Student Course Book p. 63

Listen to each sentence. Put a circle around the word you hear.

1.	(sweater) / sweaters	3.	shirt / shirts	5.	blouse / blouses	7.	coat / coats
2.	tie / ties	4.	dress / dresses	6.	belt / belts	8.	raincoat / raincoats

F. SINGULAR/PLURAL

Student Course Book p. 64

Say these words and then write them in the correct column below.

ties	raincoats	blouses	socks	pants	shoes	offices	dresses	sweaters

[s]	[z]	[ɪz]
	ties	

G. THIS RAINCOAT IS TOO LONG

Student Course Book p. 64

This	These	is	are

1. __This__ raincoat __is__ too long.   4. _____ jacket _____ too small.

2. _____ sneakers _____ too big.   5. _____ gloves _____ too tight.

3. _____ blouse _____ too large.   6. _____ suit _____ too short.

H. TOO LONG!

Student Course Book p. 64

big	large	long	short	small	tight

1. These pants are too   2. This suit is too   3. These sneakers are too

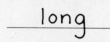
long .   _____ .   _____ .

4. This blouse is too   5. This skirt is too   6. This jacket is too

_____ .   _____ .   _____ .

Listen to each sentence. Put a check (✓) next to the appropriate picture.

1. ✓   ___   4. ___   ___

2. ___   ___   5. ___   ___

3.  ___    ___

J. THE DEPARTMENT STORE DIRECTORY   Student Course Book p. 65

1st = first	3rd = third	5th = fifth	7th = seventh	9th = ninth
2nd = second	4th = fourth	6th = sixth	8th = eighth	10th = tenth

1. Shoes are on the ___sixth___ floor.

2. Women's dresses are on the _____ floor.

3. TVs and radios are on the _____ floor.

4. Refrigerators are on the _____ floor.

5. You can eat on the _____ floor.

6. The Customer Service Counter is on the _____ floor.

7. You can buy men's suits on the _____ floor.

8. You can buy sofas and tables on the _____ floor.

9. You can buy beds on the _____ floor.

10. There are restrooms on the _____ and the _____ floors.

Floor
1st   TVs, Radios
2nd   Refrigerators, Stoves
3rd   Bedroom Furniture
4th   Customer Service Counter
5th   Restrooms, Children's Clothing
6th   Shoes, Belts, Ties
7th   Men's Clothing
8th   Women's Dresses
9th   Living Room Furniture
10th The Crown Restaurant, Restrooms

Listen and put a circle around the word you hear.

1. ⬭(1st) / 3rd

2. 5th / 9th

3. 7th / 10th

4. 6th / 5th

5. 8th / 10th

6. 4th / 5th

7. 3rd / 10th

8. 2nd / 7th

L. THAT'S FIFTEEN THIRTY-FOUR　　　　　　　　Student Course Book p. 66

Put a circle around the correct amount.

1. "That's fifteen thirty-four."　　(\$15.34) / \$153.04

2. "That's twenty-seven sixty."　　\$20.76 / \$27.60

3. "That comes to sixty-nine fifty-eight."　　\$69.58 / \$695.08

4. "That comes to five hundred twenty-six dollars and eleven cents."　　\$526.11 / \$500.27

5. "With the tax, that comes to two hundred thirty dollars and twenty cents."　　\$203.20 / \$230.20

6. "That's forty-three ninety-nine and that includes tax."　　\$43.99 / \$403.99

📼 **M. LISTENING**　　　　　　　　　　　　　　　　Student Course Book p. 66

Listen and write the amount you hear.

1. ___\$11.15___

2. _____

3. _____

4. _____

5. _____

6. _____

Write the correct amount.

1. These boots are half price.

   Now they're **$25.00** .

3. They're now 50% off.

   That comes to _____.

5. These sweaters are half price.

   That's _____.

2. The typewriters are 10% off.

   Now they're _____.

4. They're on sale. They're 10% off.

   Now that comes to _____.

6. This week they're 10% off.

   That comes to _____.

Put a circle around the correct answer.

1. I want to return this
   | (textbook) |
   | textbooks |
   .

2. I'd like to exchange these
   | fan |
   | fans |
   .

3. We want to return these
   | jean |
   | jeans |
   .

4. Do you want to return this
   | purse |
   | purses |
   ?

5. I'd like a
   | receipt |
   | receipts |
   , please.

6. Where are the
   | videogame |
   | videogames |
   ?

7. I'm looking for a
   | dressing room |
   | dressing rooms |
   .

8. I want to exchange these
   | glove |
   | gloves |
   .

| this | these | It's | They're | it | them |

1. I want to return ___these___ sneakers.

    What's the matter with _____?

    _____ too tight.

2. I'd like to return _____ purse.

    What's the matter with _____?

    _____ too big.

3. I want to return _____ workbooks.

    What's the matter with _____?

    _____ too easy.

4. I want to exchange _____ TV.

    What's the matter with _____?

    _____ too heavy.

5. He wants to return _____ coat.

    What's the matter with _____?

    _____ too short.

6. I'd like to exchange _____ books.

    What's the matter with _____?

    _____ too difficult.

Q. AT THE POST OFFICE Student Course Book p. 68

Fill in each blank with the correct word.

| aerogramme | change of address form | money order |
| stamps | registered letter | package |

1. I want to mail a ___registered letter___.

2. I'd like to buy some _____.

3. Can I file a _____ at this window?

4. I want to buy an _____, please.

5. I'd like to send a _____.

6. I'd like a _____, please.

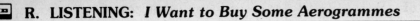

R. LISTENING: *I Want to Buy Some Aerogrammes*   Student Course Book p. 68

Listen and put the number under the appropriate picture.

_____   _____   _____

_____   1   _____

S. IS THIS PACKAGE VALUABLE?   Student Course Book p. 69

| Where How Do Is Are |

1. _____Is_____ this package valuable? Yes, it is.

2. _____ do you want to send this package? First class.

3. _____ is this letter going? To the Soviet Union.

4. _____ you want to insure this package? Yes, I do.

5. _____ these letters going to New York? Yes, they are.

6. _____ this package too big? Yes, it is.

T. LISTENING: *Where's This Package Going?*   Student Course Book p. 69

Listen and put a circle around the correct response.

1.
a. First class, please.
b. To New York.

2.
a. First class.
b. Today.

3.
a. Yes, it is.
b. No, there aren't.

4.
a. No, I don't.
b. Yes, I am.

5.
a. Thanks very much.
b. Certainly.

6.
a. Over there.
b. That's $4.00.

7.
a. No, they aren't.
b. I'd like a refund.

8.
a. All right.
b. I don't know.

Department stores in the United States are very large. They're called department stores because they have many different departments.

For example, you can buy dresses, blouses, and skirts in the Women's Clothing Department. You can buy suits, shirts, and ties in the Men's Clothing Department. Parents can buy clothing for their children in the Children's Clothing Department. Shoes, boots, and sneakers are in the Shoe Department.

Most department stores have TVs and radios in their Home Entertainment Departments. Some stores also have Appliance Departments. You can buy refrigerators, stoves, dishwashers, and other appliances there.

Do you want to read a book? Go to the Book Department. Do you want to buy a pair of earrings or a necklace? Go to the Jewelry Department. Do you want to buy some special chocolate? Go to the Gourmet Food Department.

You can buy things at special low prices when department stores have sales. Sometimes department stores even have half-price sales!

You can return things at department stores. Take your receipt to the Customer Service Department. You can exchange the things or get a refund.

In some stores, you can even eat lunch or dinner in a restaurant.

Many people like to shop in department stores. They can get almost everything they want in one place.

Answer these questions.

1. Are department stores big? _____

2. Why are they called department stores? _____

   _____

3. What can you buy in the Women's Clothing Department? _____

   _____

4. Where can you buy ties? _____

5. Can you buy children's clothing in department stores? _____

6. What kind of appliances can you buy in the Home Entertainment Department? _____

   _____

7. When can you buy things at special low prices? _____

   _____

8. Where can you return things? _____

9. Why do many people like to shop in department stores? _____

   _____

10. Where do YOU shop? What do you buy? Write about the stores you go to. . . . .

. . . .

. . . .

8

A. EXCUSE ME. WHERE'S THE CAFETERIA?

Student Course Book p. 72

| down | in | on |

1. The cafeteria is ____in____ the basement.

2. The supply room is the second door _____ the right.

3. The coffee machine is _____ the employee lounge.

4. The bathroom is _____ the hall.

5. The men's bathroom is _____ the second floor.

6. The Personnel Office is _____ the hall _____ the left.

B. WHERE'S THE PERSONNEL OFFICE?

Student Course Book p. 72

| cafeteria | Personnel Office | supply room | employee lounge | basement |

1. Excuse me. I have a job interview. Where's the _Personnel Office_?

2. My lunch break is at noon. Where's the _____?

3. This is the first floor. Take the elevator down to the _____.

4. We need someone to take inventory in the _____.

5. I'd like to take a break. Can I smoke in the _____?

C. LISTENING

Student Course Book p. 72

Sue is a new employee at the Grand
Insurance Company. Right now she's
in the Personnel Office. She's asking
some questions about the workplace.

Listen to each sentence. Put the
number in the appropriate place.

____	____
MEN'S ROOM	____
	ELEVATOR
____	
1	
PERSONNEL OFFICE	

| on Tuesday | this morning | yesterday | last week | on Monday |

Today is Friday. Tim is a new employee at the Wilson Insurance Company. He started

_this morning_____.
                            1

A lot of new employees started at the Wilson Insurance Company this week. Jane started

_____. John started _____ and Dave started _____.
        2   3   4

Steve and Bob are also new employees. They started _____.
                                                                  5

E. NO, SHE'S SHORT   Student Course Book p. 73

| light | tall | heavy | dark | thin | short | curly | straight |

1. Is Ms. Walters tall?

   No. She's __short____.

2. Is Edward heavy?

   No. He's _____.

3. Does Nancy have curly hair?

   No. She has _____ hair.

4. Does Mr. Johnson have dark brown hair?

   No. He has _____ brown hair.

5. Is he short and thin?

   No. He's _____ and _____.

6. Does she have straight, dark brown hair?

   No. She has _____, _____

   brown hair.

F. WHAT DO YOU LOOK LIKE?   Student Course Book p. 73

Describe yourself.   Are you tall? average height? short?
                      Are you thin? heavy?
                      Is your hair curly? straight?
                      Is it brown? black? blond? red? gray?

. . . .

. . . .

. . . .

G. CAN YOU SHOW ME HOW . . . ?

Put a circle around the correct word.

1. | (Pull)
    | Punch in | this chain.

2. | Press
    | Pull | this lever.

3. | Put in
    | Press | your time card.

4. | Push
    | Pull | that button.

5. | Flip
    | Put in | this switch.

6. | Pull
    | Press | those buttons.

7. | Punch in
    | Turn off | the dishwasher.

8. | Turn on
    | Punch in | this machine.

H. CAN YOU SHOW ME?

| button   time card   switch   press   chain   pull |

1. Can you show me how to punch in?

    Sure. Put in your _time card_ .

2. Can you show me how to open this?

    Yes. Push this _____ .

3. Can you show me how to start this?

    Sure. Flip this _____ .

4. Can you tell me how to turn this off?

    Sure. _____ this button.

5. Can you show me how to turn this on?

    Yes. Pull that _____ .

6. Can you show me how to turn this off?

    Yes. _____ the chain.

I. MATCHING

1. Transfer   the handle.

2. Lift   your hours here.

3. Sign   the phone.

4. List   this call, please.

5. Hang up   your name.

sign	dial	hang up	set	turn on	put	List	Flip	press

1. Could you tell me how to fill out this timesheet?

   Certainly. _____Put_____ your employee number here. _____ your hours

   and _____ your name at the bottom.

2. Can you please tell me how to transfer a call?

   Sure. _____ the red button. Then _____ the other number and

   _____ .

3. How do I use the postage machine?

   First, _____ the amount. Then, _____ the envelope in.

4. How do I light this oven?

   First, _____ a match near the hole. Then, _____ the gas.

5. Could you tell me how to use the ice cream machine?

   Sure. _____ the switch. Then _____ the button to turn the

   machine on.

K. HOW DO I TRANSFER A CALL?

Put a circle around the correct word.

1. How do I transfer a
   | telephone |
   | (call) |
   ?

5. You can use the
   | postage |
   | freight |
   machine now.

2. How do I fill out this
   | amount |
   | timesheet |
   ?

6.
   | Flip |
   | Lift |
   the handle.

3. Write your
   | employee number |
   | envelope |
   here.

7. How can I
   | light |
   | match |
   this oven?

4.
   | List |
   | Sign |
   your name.

8.
   | Hold |
   | Set |
   the amount on the machine.

Put the instructions in the correct order.   Then, complete the sentences after each question.

1. Could you show me how to use the copying machine?

    Sure. First, _____

    _____.

    Then, _____

    _____.

    Then, _____

    _____.

[2] put down the cover

[3] press the start button

[1] place the original on the glass

2. Can you show me how to lock the cash register?

    Yes. First, _____

    _____.

    Then, _____

    _____.

    Then, _____

    _____.

[ ] close the drawer

[ ] take out the tray

[ ] turn the key

3. Could you tell me how to do a credit card sale?

    Certainly. First, _____

    _____.

    Then, _____

    _____.

    Then, _____

    _____.

[ ] place the slip and card in the machine

[ ] write the date and amount on the slip

[ ] ask the customer to sign

4. Can you show me how to use the floor polishing machine?

    All right. First, _____

    _____.

    Then, _____

    _____.

    Then, _____

    _____.

[ ] go back and forth

[ ] flip the switch to turn the machine on

[ ] spray the wax on the floor

Listen and put the number under the appropriate picture.

———　　———　　———

1　　———　　———

N. WHAT DID THESE PEOPLE DO YESTERDAY?

Student Course Book p. 78

I	
He	
She	stocked the shelves.
We	
You	
They	

cleaned	operated	painted
played	stocked	washed

1. I __stocked__ the shelves.

2. Jane _____ the supply room.

3. We _____ the car.

4. Fred _____ some songs on the piano.

5. You _____ the forklift.

6. They _____ the ceiling.

blanks with the past tense forms of these words.

wash	paint	clean	stock	play	operate

1. Yesterday we ___stocked___ the shelves in the supply room.

2. The kitchen was yellow. My husband _____ it. Now it's white.

3. The housekeeper _____ all the rooms this morning.

4. Janet _____ the piano last night.

5. Mr. Johnson was a good medical technician. He _____ medical equipment for five years.

6. Doris _____ all the dishes this afternoon.

P. SHE MADE THE BEDS

Fill in the blanks with the past tense form of these words.

1. The housekeeper ___made___ the beds at 8:00 this morning.

make - made
write - wrote
give - gave

2. She _____ her name on the timesheet.

3. Our teacher _____ us a lot of homework last night.

4. The salesclerk _____ the receipt to the customer.

5. I _____ a letter to my sister on my new typewriter.

6. Mary _____ an appointment for a job interview yesterday.

7. I _____ a mistake on my homework.

8. Jennifer _____ her employee number on her time card.

Did { I / he / she / we / you / they } wash the glasses all right?

Yes, { I / he / she / we / you / they } did.

1. __Did I paint__ the ceiling all right?

Yes, __you did__. You painted it very well.

2. _____ the rooms well?

Yes, _____. She cleaned them very well.

3. _____ the shelves all right?

Yes, _____. They stocked them well.

4. _____ the reports well?

Yes, _____. He wrote them very well.

5. _____ the beds all right?

Yes, _____. You made them very well.

R. SHE'S NEW ON THE JOB

Match each question with the correct response.

1. Did she type the reports well?

2. Did she set the table okay?

3. Did she paint the room all right?

4. Did she lock the cash register?

5. Did she do his hair all right?

No, she didn't. We wanted red, but now it's yellow.

Yes, and she gave me the key.

Not really. She forgot the napkins.

Actually, she made some spelling mistakes.

Not really. She cut too much.

S. FILL IN THE BLANKS

1. What's the trouble?

   He ____cut____ my hair too short.

   ┌─────────────┐
   │ do - did   │
   │ cut - cut   │
   │ put - put   │
   │ set - set   │
   └─────────────┘

2. Did Fran help you this afternoon?

   Yes, she did. She _____ the table for lunch.

3. What did I do wrong?

   You _____ your employee number on the wrong side of the time card.

4. Did I repair the telephone all right?

   Yes. You _____ a great job!

5. Who wants the first aid kit?

   Fred. He _____ his finger on his machine.

T. SAY THESE WORDS!

Say these words and then write them in the correct columns below.

cleaned	cooked	inspected	operated	painted	played
repaired	stocked	typed	washed	wanted	

[t]	[d]	[ɪd]
	cleaned	

U. LISTENING

Listen to each sentence. Put a circle around the correct word.

1. (yesterday)
   every day

2. yesterday
   every day

3. yesterday
   every day

4. yesterday
   every day

5. yesterday
   every day

6. yesterday
   every day

V. MATCHING

Match the safety equipment with the correct word.

1. helmet   clothes

2. safety glasses   head

3. gloves   eyes

4. hairnet   hands

5. labcoat   hair

W. WHERE'S YOUR HELMET?

Put a circle around the correct word.

1. Where's your (helmet) / glasses ?

2. Take these hairnet / gloves to Mr. Hill.

3. Where are your labcoat / uniforms ?

4. Please get some uniform / safety glasses .

5. Where are your helmet / keys ?

6. My time card / gloves ? Uh . . . I forgot them.

X. LISTENING

Listen to each sentence. Put a circle around the correct word.

1. (helmet) / helmets

2. key / keys

3. box / boxes

4. labcoat / labcoats

5. bed / beds

6. hairnet / hairnets

Y. I DID THAT ALREADY

Student Course Book p. 81

do	make	set	wash	type	use		it	them

1. Please ___wash___ the car.

   I did that already. I _____ _____ this afternoon.

2. Please _____ the tables.

   We did that already. We _____ _____ about a half hour ago.

3. Could you _____ these letters, please?

   I did that already. I _____ _____ yesterday afternoon.

4. Could you please _____ your bed?

   I did that already. I _____ _____ this morning.

5. Please _____ your homework.

   We did that already. We _____ _____ an hour ago.

6. Please _____ the floor polishing machine tonight.

   We did that already. We _____ _____ two hours ago.

Z. I'M FREE NOW

Student Course Book p. 81

Put a circle around the correct word.

1. (I'm) / I was free now.

2. Joe sweeps / swept the floor already.

3. We do / did that already.

4. She forgets / forgot it. It's in her car.

5. Please give / gave this box to Hank.

6. They help / helped me last week.

7. Call me. My number is / was 588-0038.

8. He punches / punched in an hour ago.

9. Pull / Pulled the handle.

10. I leave / left my keys at home today.

Yesterday afternoon, Kenji started his first job in the United States. He's a waiter at the Expressway Restaurant.

Kenji did many new things on his first day at the restaurant. He wrote his name and employee number on his time card and punched in. He tried on his waiter's uniform. It fit very well. He studied the menu and talked with the other waiters and waitresses.

The restaurant opened at 5:00. The customers were very nice. Kenji was afraid his English was poor, but he didn't make any mistakes! He talked with the customers, took their orders, and he served the food very quickly. He even used the cash register.   Kenji was busy all evening.

The restaurant closed at 12:00. Kenji and the other employees cleaned up. They swept the floor, cleaned the tables and chairs, and set the tables for the next day. At 1:00 A.M., they finished work and went home.

Today is Kenji's second day on the job. He's punching in, but something is wrong! The machine isn't working. The manager is looking at Kenji's time card. What's the matter? Kenji made one small mistake. He forgot to punch out last night!

Answer the questions.

1. When did Kenji start his new job? _____

2. What's his job? _____

3. What did he write on his time card? _____

_____

4. How did his uniform fit? _____

5. What did Kenji do before the restaurant opened? _____

_____

6. What time did the restaurant open? _____

7. Did Kenji make any mistakes when he talked with the customers? _____

8. Did he use the cash register? _____

9. What did Kenji and the other employees do from 12:00 to 1:00? _____

_____

10. What did Kenji do wrong last night? _____

9

A. WHAT DO THEY WANT TO DO?

Student Course Book p. 84

| I
We
You
They | } **want** to see a movie. | He
She | } **wants** to see a movie. |

| go to a museum | go skiing | watch TV |
| have a picnic | go swimming | see a movie |

1. What do you want to do today?

I want to have a picnic.

2. What do they want to do today?

_____

3. What does Charles want to do?

_____

4. What does Sally want to do today?

_____

5. What do you want to do tonight?

_____

6. What do Bob and Karen want to do?

_____

B. WHAT'S THE WEATHER LIKE TODAY?

Student Course Book p. 84

1.

It's sunny.

2.

_____

3.

_____

4.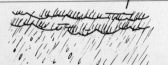

_____

5.

_____

6.

_____

76

C. MATCHING

Draw a line to the appropriate words for each group.

1. It's snowing. Do you want to   stay home?
2. It's cold. Do you want to   have a picnic?
3. It's sunny. Do you want to   go skiing?

4. It's raining. We should   go swimming.
5. It's hot. We want to   go skating.
6. It's cold. We can   take umbrellas.

7. It's cloudy. We should   go to the zoo.
8. It's sunny. I'd like to   buy an umbrella.
9. It's raining. He wants to   go to a museum.

D. THEY DON'T WANT TO . . .

They don't want to . . .	Why?
1. They don't want to have a picnic.	They had a picnic _____ yesterday.
2. Jessica doesn't want to go to the beach today.	_____ last weekend.
3. Norman doesn't want to play tennis right now.	_____ this morning.
4. Barbara and I don't want to drive to the city tonight.	_____ last night.
5. I don't want to go sailing.	_____ last Sunday.
6. He doesn't want to play basketball right now.	_____ yesterday afternoon.
7. Rich and John don't want to go jogging now.	_____ a little while ago.
8. We don't want to go to the zoo again.	_____ last Tuesday morning.

⊡ E. LISTENING

Listen to each sentence. Put the number next to the appropriate picture.

 ____

 1

 ____

 ____

 ____

 ____

F. WHAT'S THE WEATHER FORECAST?

Fill in the blanks with the best answer.

| hot   cloudy |

1. Let's go to the beach.

    It's going to be __hot__.

| rain   snow |

2. Let's go skating. The newspaper

    says it's going to _____.

| cloudy   sunny |

3. Let's see a movie. I heard it's

    going to be _____.

| cold   sunny |

4. Let's go sailing. The news says

    it's going to be _____.

| rain   be sunny |

5. Let's play basketball inside today. The

    radio says it's going to _____.

| nice   very cold |

6. Let's do something outdoors today.

    It's going to be _____.

G. MATCHING

Draw a line to the correct words for each group.

1. I read the forecast   on the radio.
2. We heard it   the Weather Information Number.
3. George called   in the newspaper.

4. My sister saw the weather forecast on   the Weather Information Number.
5. Karen and Bill read the forecast in   TV.
6. We should call   the paper.

Helen doesn't want to go out with Norman. Write her excuses.
Then practice the dialog with another student.

Hello, Helen. This is Norman. Do you want to go for a bike ride tomorrow morning?
    I'm afraid I can't. I have to go to the dentist. . . . .
Do you want to go for a bike ride Sunday afternoon?
    I'm afraid I can't. . . . .
How about next weekend?
    I'm afraid I can't. . . . .
Do you want to have dinner tomorrow?
    I'm afraid I can't. . . . .
Do you want to have dinner next Monday?
    I'm afraid I can't. . . . .
That's too bad.
    Maybe some other time.
Okay.

I. I'M AFRAID I CAN'T

Fill in the blanks.

I He She We You They } can't.	I We You } have to work late. He She } has to

1. Can Tom go dancing tonight?

    No, **he can't**.
    He has to baby-sit.

2. Can Maria go see a play with me tonight?

    No, _____. _____ study for an exam.

3. Can they go to a concert this weekend?

    No, _____. _____ visit their aunt.

4. Can Fred go to the zoo with us tomorrow?

    No, _____. _____ do his homework.

5. Can you and your wife come to dinner Friday night?

    No, _____. _____ go to Philadelphia.

6. Can Don go to New York with us this weekend?

    No, _____. _____ work this weekend.

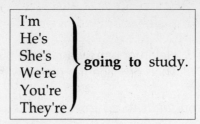

I'm
He's
She's
We're
You're
They're
} **going to** study.

1. What are you going to do tonight?

We're going to study.

2. What's Joe going to do tomorrow?

_____

3. What are Mr. and Mrs. Smith going to do?

_____

4. What's she going to do this weekend?

_____

5. What are you going to do this afternoon?

_____

6. What's your brother going to do this morning?

_____

7. What are they going to do today?

_____

8. What am I going to do next year?

. . . .

K.   THE CLAYTON FAMILY IS GOING TO BE VERY BUSY!   Student Course Book p. 88

Mary and Bob Clayton and their children, Michael and Jane, are going to be very busy this week. They're going to do a lot of things. This is their calendar for the week.

MONDAY	TUESDAY	WEDNESDAY	THURSDAY	FRIDAY	SATURDAY	SUNDAY
JANE: GO TO THE DENTIST! 9:00	MICHAEL AND BOB: FIX THE DISHWASHER!	BOB AND MARY: SEE FRED'S STORY 8:00	MICHAEL: RETURN BOOKS TO THE LIBRARY!	JANE: BABY-SIT 7:30	EVERYBODY: CLEAN THE GARAGE! CLEAN THE YARD!	EVERYBODY: VISIT AUNT DORIS IN THE HOSPITAL!

1. What's Jane going to do on Monday morning? _She's going to go to the dentist._

2. What are Bob and Michael going to do on Tuesday? _____
_____

3. What are Bob and Mary going to do on Wednesday evening? _____
_____

4. What's Michael going to do on Thursday? _____

5. What's Jane going to do on Friday evening? _____

6. What's everybody going to do on Saturday? _____
_____

7. What are they all going to do on Sunday? _____
_____

L.   HAVE A GOOD WEEKEND!   Student Course Book p. 88

Fill in the blanks. Then practice the dialogs with another student.

| want to   going to   have to |

1. What are you ___going to___ do this weekend?

    I'm _____ go to the beach. How about you?

    I don't know. I _____ go to the mountains, but I can't.

    I _____ study for an exam.

    Well, have a good weekend!

    You, too.

2. Do you _____ see a movie tomorrow night?

    I'm afraid I can't. I _____ clean my house.

    How about tomorrow night? What are you _____ do tomorrow night?

    Nothing. Do you _____ get together tomorrow night?

    Yes. What do you _____ do?

    I _____ see a movie.

    Okay.

How **was** your weekend?   It **was** very nice.

delicious   difficult   easy   cold   sunny

1. How was dinner last night?

    I really enjoyed it. __It was delicious._____

2. How was the weather in Florida?

    _____ We went to the beach every day.

3. How was your exam?

    I'm worried. _____

4. How was your homework?

    I didn't have any trouble with it. _____

5. How was the weather?

    _____ We skated yesterday.

Put a circle around the correct word.

1. Let's visit | (Aunt) / Uncle | Barbara.

5. Give your | grandfather / grandmother | his paper.

2. This is my son and his | husband / wife | .

6. This is my sister's new | wife / husband | .

3. My | wife / son | forgot her book.

7. This is my | father / parents | .

4. These are my | aunt / children | .

8. This is my son and his | parents / children | .

O. HOW WAS YOUR WEEKEND?

Student Course Book p. 89

Fill in the blanks. Then practice the dialogs with another student.

| was | did | | played | cleaned | visited | went | wrote |

1. How ___**was**___ your weekend?

    It _____ okay.

    What _____ you do?

    I _____ skating.

    Oh. Where _____ you go?

    To the lake.

2. What _____ you do last night?

    I _____ basketball with

    some friends.

    How _____ the game?

    It _____ fun. _____

    YOU do anything special last night?

    Not really. I _____ some letters.

3. _____ you do anything special

    last weekend?

    Yes. I _____ to a party.

    How _____ it?

    It _____ nice. What

    _____ YOU do last weekend?

    I _____ my aunt in New York.

4. How _____ your weekend?

    It _____ excellent. I

    _____ skiing. What

    _____ YOU do?

    Nothing special. I _____

    my apartment.

P. WHERE WERE YOU?

Student Course Book p. 90

| I He She It } **was** at the party. | We You They } **were** at the party. |

I ___**was**___ with Diane and Jane yesterday evening. We _____ at Fred's
                1   2

party from 10:00 to midnight. Jeff _____ there. Debbie and Pamela _____
                                                          3   4

there, too. I don't think Gloria _____ there, but a lot of people _____ at the
                                                        5   6

party! The food _____ delicious. The music _____ good for dancing. It
                                  7   8

_____ fun! Where _____ you?
        9   10

Put a circle around the correct word.

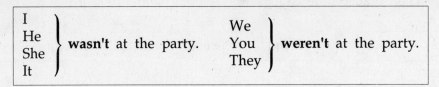

It ⟨**was** / were⟩[1] Janet's birthday last night. She wanted to do something special. She called her

friends Melissa and Jane, but they ⟨wasn't / weren't⟩[2] home. She wanted to talk to her friend Carlos, but

he ⟨wasn't / weren't⟩[3] home. She called her sister, Mary, but she ⟨was / were⟩[4] out somewhere. Janet

couldn't even find her dog. It ⟨was / were⟩[5] outdoors somewhere.

She went to her aunt and uncle's house. They ⟨wasn't / weren't⟩[6] home. She then went to visit her

grandmother and grandfather. She ⟨was / were⟩[7] sure they ⟨was / were⟩[8] home.

Janet ⟨was / were⟩[9] right! They ⟨were / weren't⟩[10] home! And, surprise! Everybody else was at their

home, too. Melissa and Jane ⟨was / were⟩[11] there. Carlos, Mary, and other friends ⟨was / were⟩[12] there.

Of course, her grandparents ⟨was / were⟩[13] there. Even her dog ⟨was / wasn't⟩[14] there. It ⟨was / were⟩[15]

an excellent party!

R. WHERE DID YOU GO LAST WEEKEND? span style>Student Course Book p. 90

Fill in each blank with the correct word.

Who	What	Where	How

1. __Where__ did you go last weekend? We went to the beach.

2. _____ much was that textbook? It was $8.50.

3. _____ did you go to the game with? My friend Tom.

4. _____ movie do you want to see? Let's see "Picnic."

5. _____ did you do yesterday? We stayed home and studied.

6. _____ did you visit in Rome? My aunt and uncle.

7. _____ was the weather like? It was very hot.

8. _____ was that book? It was interesting.

9. _____ many hours did you work? Eight.

10. _____ was that on the phone? My sister.

S. LISTENING Student Course Book p. 90

Listen to each question. Put a circle around the correct response.

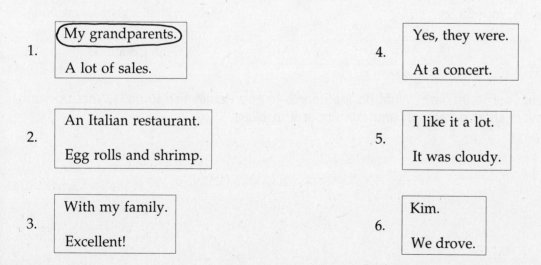

1. (My grandparents.) / A lot of sales.

2. An Italian restaurant. / Egg rolls and shrimp.

3. With my family. / Excellent!

4. Yes, they were. / At a concert.

5. I like it a lot. / It was cloudy.

6. Kim. / We drove.

85

Fill in the blanks.

I	
We	}like to run.
You	
They	

He	
She	}likes to run.
It	

1. I ___like___ ___to___ ___knit___
children's clothes.

2. My grandchildren _____

_____ _____ in Garden Lake.

3. Ellen _____ _____

_____ novels.

4. We _____ _____ _____
tennis.

5. They _____ _____

_____ every morning.

6. Charlie _____ _____

_____ basketball every afternoon.

What do you like to do in your free time? What do the people in your family like to do? What do your friends like to do? Write a short paragraph and talk about it in class.

. . . .

. . . .

. . . .

. . . .

. . . .

. . . .

Put a circle around the word that doesn't belong.

1. textbook   (types)   novels   biographies

2. rivers   mountains   lakes   ballgames

3. uncle   sister   husband   son

4. clean   run   walk   jog

5. evening   afternoon   special   morning

6. swim   paint   read   fun

7. cakes   restaurant   cookies   bread

8. people   sweater   blouse   shirt

W. *LIKE* OR *LIKE TO*?   Student Course Book pp. 92-93

I We You They } **like** comedies.	I We You They } **like to** go to the movies.
He She } **likes** comedies.	He She } **likes to** go to the movies.

1. Ned and I | like / (like to) | go sailing.   6. Kevin | likes / likes to | Greek restaurants.

2. They | like / like to | mysteries.   7. I | like / like to | friendly people.

3. Do you | like / like to | jog along the lake?   8. Jackie | likes / likes to | bake bread.

4. Does Gloria | like / like to | play golf?   9. We don't | like / like to | westerns.

5. Glen doesn't | like / like to | work late.   10. I | like / like to | see adventure movies.

Bobby Henderson is studying at a college in New York. Last weekend, he had to study for an exam, but Bobby didn't really want to study. He just wanted to have fun. On Friday night, he went dancing. On Saturday morning, he played tennis with his friend John. On Saturday afternoon, his friends called and they all had a picnic together in the park. On Saturday evening, he went to a party at Glen's apartment. It was fun. He went to bed at about midnight.

On Sunday, the weather was bad. It was cold and cloudy. It was a good day to study, but Bobby didn't want to. Instead, he went to see a movie. The title of the film was *Cloudy Monday*. Bobby didn't like it. It was a comedy, and he doesn't like comedies very much.

Finally, on Sunday night, he studied for his exam. He studied from 6:00 in the evening to 1:00 in the morning.

On Monday morning, Bobby went to school and took the exam. He was very tired, and he didn't do very well. Bobby was really sorry. He didn't study for the test. He just wanted to have fun.

Answer the questions.

1. What did Bobby have to do last weekend? _____

   _____

2. Did he want to study? _____

3. What did he want to do? _____

4. What did he do on Friday night? _____

5. What did Bobby and his friends do on Saturday afternoon? _____

   _____

6. Where did he go on Saturday evening? _____

   _____

7. What was the weather like on Sunday? _____

   _____

8. Where did Bobby go on Sunday? _____

9. What was the title of the film? _____

   _____

10. When did Bobby study for the exam? _____

11. What did he do on Monday morning? _____

12. Did Bobby do well on the exam? _____

13. Why was he sorry? _____

14. Do YOU like to study for exams? When do you study? . . . .

    . . . .

    . . . .

A. Put a circle around the correct answer.

Example   I
has to
having to
(have to)
work late.

1.
We
It's
It
going to be cold.

2.   Kim
like
read
want
an interesting book.

3.   Please
cleaned
cleans
clean
this room well.

4.   Did John
did
does
do
a good job?

5.   I forgot it
last week
this Friday
tomorrow night
.

6.
How
Does
Where's
this letter going?

7.   I'd like to buy
them
those
that
pajamas.

8.
Dress
Earring
Gloves
are on the second floor.

9.   Where are your
company
glasses
timesheet
?

10.   Do you want to go
tomorrow
yesterday
last night
?

11.   What
has
do
did
Sally do wrong?

B. Fill in the blanks.

Example   What's the matter with that tie?

_____It's_____ too short.

1.   Did he repair the TV all right?

He repaired _____ very well.

2.   They _____ jogging yesterday.

3.   He's short, _____ gray hair.

4.   I'm looking _____ a new dress.

5.   I'd _____ to buy this TV.

6.   Did I type the reports okay?

You typed _____ very well.

7.   His office is _____ the hall.

8.   Can you come with us?

I'm afraid I _____.

9.   I have _____ study tonight.

10.   It's going to _____ cloudy.

11.   The cafeteria is _____ the right.

12.   How was your weekend?

It _____ nice.

13.   Can you help me _____ a minute?

14.   Do you want to try _____ another shirt?

C. Put a circle around the correct word.

Example | Where's / (What's) | the matter with it?

1. What / How | was your weekend?

2. Who / What | did I do wrong?

3. When / Who | do you go jogging with?

4. How / What | kind of music do you like?

5. How / Where | are the stamps?

6. When / What | are you going to do tonight?

7. What / Where | is this package going?

8. How / What | do you want to do today?

9. Which / How | do those boots fit?

D. Listen to each sentence. Put a circle around the letter of the correct response.

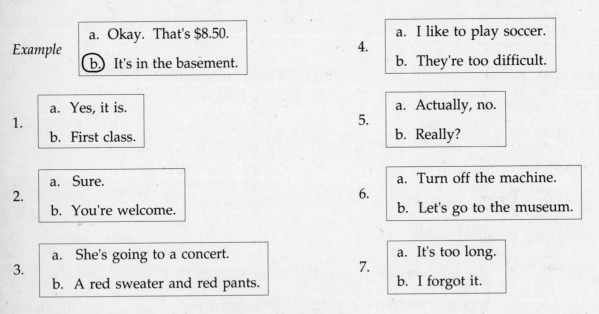

Example
a. Okay. That's $8.50.
(b.) It's in the basement.

1.
a. Yes, it is.
b. First class.

2.
a. Sure.
b. You're welcome.

3.
a. She's going to a concert.
b. A red sweater and red pants.

4.
a. I like to play soccer.
b. They're too difficult.

5.
a. Actually, no.
b. Really?

6.
a. Turn off the machine.
b. Let's go to the museum.

7.
a. It's too long.
b. I forgot it.

E. Put a circle around the word that doesn't belong.

Example	rain	sunny	(jazz)	cloudy
1.	jacket	camera	shirt	blouse
2.	long	black	gray	white
3.	boots	shoes	belts	sneakers
4.	son	uncle	wife	singer
5.	baseball	movie	tennis	golf

TAPE SCRIPTS FOR LISTENING EXERCISES

Page 3 Exercise D
Listen and write the missing letters.
1. B-R-E-N-N-E-R
2. B-A-R-B-A-R-A
3. C-L-A-Y-T-O-N
4. S-M-I-T-H
5. K-W-A-N
6. K-E-L-T-O-N
7. P-E-T-E-R-S-O-N
8. M-I-C-H-A-E-L
9. H-U-S-B-A-N-D
10. J-E-S-S-I-C-A

Page 4 Exercise E
Listen and put a circle around the right answer.
1. Could you spell that please?
2. What's your first name?
3. What's your name?
4. And your last name?
5. What's your first name?
6. Could you spell that, please?

Page 5 Exercise H
Listen and write the number of the address you hear.
1. Six Maple Street
2. Eleven Pond Avenue
3. Fourteen Howard Street
4. Three Main Road
5. Seventeen Summer Street
6. Eighteen twelve Central Avenue

Page 5 Exercise I
Listen and write the numbers you hear.
1. 543-6905
2. 249-1986
3. 673-5220
4. 946-1682
5. 892-0677
6. 439-1908

Page 6 Exercise J
Listen and circle the right answer.
1. What's your address?
2. What's your telephone number?
3. What's your name?
4. What's your address?
5. What's your phone number?
6. What's your last name?

Page 9 Exercise O
Listen and circle the best answer.
1. Where are you from?
2. Are you Australian?
3. Are you from New York?
4. What's your phone number?
5. What's your first name?
6. Are you Mrs. Chen?
7. Is your name Sanchez?
8. Where are they from?

Page 11 Exercise C
Listen and circle the answer to the question.
1. Is this 547-2055?
2. Is this 498-5930?
3. Is this 622-6835?
4. Is this 356-9472?
5. Is this 285-2841?

Page 12 Exercise D
Listen and write the missing numbers.
1. A. I'd like the number of Donald Hicks.
   B. Just a moment . . . the number is 573-5108.
2. A. What's the telephone number please?
   B. 963-6882.
3. A. I'd like your telephone number.
   B. My number is 527-5382.
4. A. What's your telephone number?
   B. It's 623-4406.
5. A. And what's your telephone number please?
   B. My number is 572-4329.
6. A. I'd like the number of Peter Craven.
   B. Just a moment . . . the number is 248-9206.

Page 17 Exercise M
Listen to the conversation and choose the correct picture.
1. A. What's Jeff doing?
   B. He's cooking dinner.
2. A. What are you doing?
   B. We're doing our homework.
3. A. Where is Mrs. Chen going?
   B. She's going to the library.
4. A. What's Jane doing?
   B. She's looking for her car.
5. A. What are Kathy and Bob doing?
   B. They're dancing.
6. A. Where are they going?
   B. They're going to the mall.

Page 21 Exercise D
Listen to each conversation. Put a circle around the number you hear.
1. A. Which bus goes downtown?
   B. Number 29.
2. A. Which train goes to Westville?
   B. Number 43.
3. A. Does this bus go to the park?
   B. No, take Number 35.
4. A. Does this bus go to New York?
   B. No, take Number 20.
5. A. What's your address?
   B. 68 Central Avenue.
6. A. Which bus goes to Broadway?
   B. Take Bus Number 72.
7. A. What's your address?
   B. It's 58 Grand Avenue.
8. A. What's your address?
   B. It's 4936 Center Street.
9. A. Is there a post office nearby?
   B. Yes. It's at 4560 River Street.
10. A. Is there a supermarket nearby?
    B. Yes. It's at 8646 Main Avenue.
11. A. What's his address?
    B. 4028 Broadway.
12. A. Where is the Riverside Hotel?
    B. It's at 5764 River Boulevard.

Page 22 Exercise F
Listen to each question. Put a circle around the correct answer.
1. Does this plane go to Atlanta?
2. Does this train stop at Broadway?
3. Is this the Number 4 bus?
4. Is this 429-9292?
5. Does this bus go to Miami?
6. Is this the downtown train?
7. Does this bus stop at the shopping mall?
8. Does this train go uptown?

Page 24 Exercise H

Listen to each sentence. Put the number of the sentence in the correct box.

1. The museum is between the bus station and the clinic.
2. The hospital is next to the department store.
3. The gas station is across from the clinic.
4. The park is across from the post office.
5. The supermarket is next to the hotel.

Page 26 Exercise M

Listen to each conversation. Put a circle around the correct answer.

1. A. Take Bus Number 25 to Summer Street.
   B. Sorry. Did you say Bus Number 23?
2. A. Walk that way two blocks.
   B. Sorry. Did you say two blocks?
3. A. Drive that way twelve miles.
   B. Did you say twelve miles?
4. A. Turn left on Third Street.
   B. I'm sorry. Did you say Fifth Street?
5. A. Go five blocks and turn right.
   B. Did you say five blocks?
6. A. Turn right on Grand Avenue and go seven blocks.
   B. Did you say eleven blocks?
7. A. Take the Fourth Street bus and get off at Main Street.
   B. Sorry. Did you say the First Street bus?
8. A. Take the Expressway and get off at Exit 24.
   B. Did you say Exit 24?
9. A. The post office is at forty-two twenty-two Broadway.
   B. Forty-two twenty-two?
10. A. My telephone number is 276-1274.
    B. Sorry. Did you say 276-1264?

Page 27 Exercise O

Write the number of the location you hear.

1. The library is on Third Street, across from the clinic.
2. The hotel is on Second Street, between the park and the theater.
3. The museum is on Main Street, around the corner from the bank.
4. The drug store is on Main Street, next to the post office.
5. The gas station is on Maple Street, next to the supermarket.

Page 30 Exercise F

Listen and write the number you hear.

Example   Is this Bus Number 56?
1. Get off at Exit 23.
2. Take the Expressway and get off at Exit 68.
3. Drive ten blocks that way.
4. The Number 34 bus goes to New York.
5. My address is sixty-two eighteen Riverside Drive.
6. The number is 547-2155.
7. Mr. Chen's address is forty-six nineteen Central Avenue.
8. Is this 965-3280?
9. My telephone number is 673-5520.

Page 32 Exercise C

Listen to each conversation. Put the number in the appropriate place.

1. A. Is there a stove in the kitchen?
   B. Yes, there is.
2. A. Can you describe the living room?
   B. Yes. It has a fireplace and a large window.
3. A. Are there cabinets in the dining room?
   B. No, there aren't.
4. A. How many windows are there in the bedroom?
   B. Two.
5. A. Where's Mary?
   B. She's taking a shower.

Page 33 Exercise F

Listen to each sentence. Put the number under the appropriate box.

1. The rent is four hundred thirty dollars.
2. The rent is two hundred twenty-five dollars.
3. I have a three-bedroom apartment for you. The rent is five hundred eighty dollars.
4. The rent is six hundred fifty dollars plus utilities.
5. I have an apartment for you. It has two bedrooms.

Page 33 Exercise G

Listen to each conversation. Write the number you hear.

1. A. How much is the rent?
   B. It's six hundred dollars a month.
2. A. How much is the gas?
   B. About fifty dollars a month.
3. A. About how much is the electricity?
   B. Hmm. About sixty dollars a month.
4. A. And how many parking spaces are there?
   B. Hmm. Let's see. I think there are fifty.
5. A. What's the parking fee?
   B. It's one hundred dollars a month.
6. A. What's the address?
   B. Two hundred eighty-four Central Avenue.

Page 34 Exercise L

Listen to each sentence. Put a check under the appropriate picture.

1. A. Where do you want this table?
   B. Put it in the kitchen.
2. A. What are you looking for?
   B. The plants.
3. A. Where do you want these pictures?
   B. Put them in the living room.
4. A. I'm afraid there aren't any more bananas.
   B. There aren't?
5. A. I'm looking for a lamp.
   B. This lamp?
6. A. What are you looking for?
   B. An egg.

Page 35 Exercise O

Listen to each sentence. Put a circle around the word you hear.

1. There aren't any more tomatoes.
2. Is there a refrigerator in the kitchen?
3. Are there any eggs in the refrigerator?
4. I'm looking for a cookie.
5. I'll get some more bananas when I go to the supermarket.
6. And how many apples are there?
7. I'm afraid there aren't any more oranges.
8. There aren't any more chairs.
9. Do you want to see the neighborhood?
10. There are two elevators in the building.

Page 36 Exercise S

Listen to each sentence. Put a circle around the correct answer.

1. I'm sorry. Did you say eight?
2. The rice is in Aisle B.
3. It's in Aisle M.
4. Sorry. Did you say G?
5. Is there butter in Aisle 3?
6. There are nine potatoes in the refrigerator.
7. The carrots? They're in Aisle A.
8. I'm looking for Aisle 10C.
9. I'm sorry. Did you say eighteen?

Page 40 Exercise F

Listen to each sentence. Put a circle around the correct day or time.

1. Can you come in for an interview today at two o'clock?
2. Can you come in on Thursday at ten thirty?
3. Can you come in on Friday at three o'clock?
4. Hmm. How about Tuesday at nine thirty?
5. Can you come in on Monday at eleven o'clock?
6. Can you come in for an interview on Tuesday at two o'clock?

Page 40 Exercise G

Listen and write the time you hear.

1. I have an interview today at eight thirty.
2. Peter's interview is at one o'clock.
3. She has an interview at twelve thirty.
4. Can you come in for an interview at three thirty today?
5. Can you come in at nine?
6. My interview's at two thirty.

Page 44 Exercise R

Listen to each conversation. Write the number you hear.

1. A. May I ask about the salary?
   B. Yes. It's six dollars an hour.
2. A. What's the salary?
   B. It's five dollars an hour.
3. A. What time is the lunch break?
   B. At twelve thirty.
4. A. Can you tell me the salary?
   B. Sure. It's two hundred dollars a week.
5. A. May I ask about the salary?
   B. Yes. It's fourteen thousand dollars a year.
6. A. What time is lunch?
   B. At twelve noon.
7. A. Can you tell me about the work schedule?
   B. Yes. Hours are from eight to four thirty.
8. A. May I ask about the schedule?
   B. Sure. It's from seven to four.
9. A. What's the schedule?
   B. From nine to five thirty.

Page 44 Exercise T

Listen to each sentence. Put a circle around the correct answer.

1. The salary is five dollars an hour.
2. Lunch is at twelve o'clock.
3. The salary is two hundred thirty dollars a week.
4. The salary is four dollars an hour.
5. The lunch break is at eleven.
6. The salary is fifty dollars a day.
7. The break is at three thirty.
8. Lunch is one dollar.

Page 46 Exercise B

Listen to each sentence. Write the correct number under the appropriate picture.

1. I have a headache.
2. Jim has a stomachache.
3. I'm sorry to hear that Charles has an earache.
4. He has a sore throat today.
5. Rick has a backache.
6. Jessica has a toothache.

Page 48 Exercise I

Listen to each question. Write the time you hear.

1. Can you come in at ten fifteen?
2. Can you come in today at three forty-five?
3. Can you come in tomorrow at nine thirty?
4. Can you come in tomorrow morning at eleven fifteen?
5. Can you come in tomorrow morning at nine forty-five?
6. Can you come in for an interview tomorrow at two forty-five?

Page 49 Exercise J

Listen to each sentence. Put the number under the appropriate box.

1. I have a terrible toothache.
2. My ears are ringing.
3. My foot hurts.
4. My neck is stiff.
5. I'm feeling very dizzy.

Page 52 Exercise S

Listen to the directions. Put the number under the appropriate medicine bottle.

1. Take one pill four times a day.
2. Take three tablets twice a day.
3. Be sure to take one capsule three times a day.
4. Follow the directions. Take one teaspoon twice a day.
5. Be sure to follow the directions. Take two capsules two times a day.
6. Be sure to follow the directions on the label. Take one pill once a day.

Page 54 Exercise F

Listen and write the number you hear.

Example   The salary is three hundred dollars a week.
1. Take three capsules a day.
2. The lunch break is at twelve forty-five.
3. His salary is thirteen thousand dollars a year.
4. A. How long did you work there?
   B. Two years.
5. The address is thirty-four twenty-one Park Lane.
6. The medicine is in Aisle eleven.
7. That apartment has four bedrooms.
8. Her appointment is at eleven fifteen.
9. The rent is one thousand twenty-five dollars a month.

Page 56 Exercise E

Listen to each sentence. Put a circle around the word you hear.

1. I'm looking for a sweater.
2. Ties are over there.
3. I'm looking for a long-sleeved shirt.
4. Dresses are in the front of the store.
5. I have some nice blouses for you.
6. Here you are . . . two black belts.
7. There's a brown coat over there.
8. Raincoats are on that rack.

Page 58 Exercise I

Listen to each sentence. Put a check next to the appropriate picture.

1. This jacket is too short.
2. These sneakers are too tight.
3. This skirt is too large.
4. I think these gloves are too big.
5. I think that suit is too small.

Page 59 Exercise K

Listen and put a circle around the word you hear.

1. Bedroom furniture is on the first floor.
2. You can eat lunch on the ninth floor.
3. Women's clothing is on the tenth floor.
4. I think the restaurant is on the fifth floor.
5. Restrooms are on the eighth floor.
6. TVs and radios are on the fourth floor.
7. Suits are on the third floor near the elevator.
8. Men's clothing is on the seventh floor.

Page 59 Exercise M

Listen and write the amount you hear.

1. That's eleven dollars and fifteen cents.
2. That comes to sixty-four dollars and thirty cents.
3. That's forty-three fifty.
4. With the tax, that comes to seventy-eight sixty-four.
5. That comes to one hundred thirty-eight dollars and forty-three cents and that includes tax.
6. That comes to two hundred seventy-nine dollars and sixty-three cents.

Page 62 Exercise R
Listen and put the number under the appropriate picture.

1. I want to buy some aerogrammes.
2. I'd like some stamps, please.
3. I want to send a registered letter.
4. I'd like to mail a package to Japan.
5. Where can I buy a money order?
6. Where do I file this change of address form?

Page 62 Exercise T
Listen and put a circle around the letter of the correct response.

1. Where's this package going?
2. How do you want to send this letter?
3. Is this package valuable?
4. Do you want to insure this letter?
5. Can you help me?
6. Where can I buy stamps?
7. Are these letters going to Miami?
8. How do you want to send this package?

Page 64 Exercise C
Listen to each sentence. Put the number in the appropriate place.

1. Your office is the first door on the left.
2. The ladies' room is down the hall, the last door on the left.
3. The supply room is down the hall, the last door on the right.
4. The cafeteria is down the hall, across from the men's room.
5. The employee lounge is on the left between your office and the men's room.
6. The manager's office is the first door on the right.

Page 69 Exercise M
Listen and put the number under the appropriate picture.

1. Close the drawer.
2. Write the date and amount on the slip.
3. Spray the wax on the floor.
4. Place the slip and credit card in the machine.
5. Ask the customer to sign the slip.
6. Press the start button.

Page 72 Exercise U
Listen to each sentence. Put a circle around the correct word.

1. The secretary typed the letters well.
2. She cleans her room well.
3. My mother washes my sweaters.
4. We operated that machine all morning.
5. Fred gives excellent reports.
6. Barbara made a very nice lunch.

Page 73 Exercise X
Listen to each sentence. Put a circle around the correct word.

1. Sorry. I left it at home.
2. You're required to have them at all times.
3. Can I help you carry them?
4. Where did you put it?
5. Where do you want them?
6. I'm afraid I left it in the bathroom.

Page 78 Exercise E
Listen to each sentence. Put the number next to the appropriate picture.

1. We went skiing last weekend.
2. They went to the zoo yesterday.
3. Nancy played golf with Jimmy last Saturday.
4. Jeff went swimming this afternoon.
5. Last Monday, I went to the museum.
6. Yesterday afternoon, he drove to the mountains.

Page 85 Exercise S
Listen to each question. Put a circle around the correct response.

1. Who did you see at the shopping mall?
2. What did you eat last night?
3. How was lunch yesterday?
4. Where were your children?
5. What was the weather like in Spain?
6. Who did you go to the store with?

Page 90 Exercise D
Listen to each sentence. Put a circle around the letter of the correct response.

Example Where's the men's bathroom?
1. How do you want to send this package?
2. Could you help me for a minute?
3. What's she going to do tonight?
4. What's the matter with those books?
5. Did I wash the clothes all right?
6. What do you want to do this afternoon?
7. Where's your homework?